The
Chronicles
of
Kismah

SCOTT HUMPHREYS

Strangford Publications
Northern Ireland

"The I that Listens is the
I that I admire."

Kismah

First Published in the UK
By Strangford Publications
Northern Ireland

Design: Luke Alexander

ISBN 978-0-9576671-1-2

Contents

Introduction

A Voice from the Future

During a period of my adult life I heard a clear voice, not in the sense one might describe as a communication but more of a statement or exclamation. Perhaps I should have been inclined to discard it as being nothing more than a figment of my imagination, but there was often something intriguing or profound in the words it spoke that compelled me to take notice. It lasted for around seven years and I use to write the phrases down in a little book.

Although I do not confess to have understood the significance of what I was hearing, many of the remarks seemed to make sense many years later when events in my life had changed. However there is one phrase that stood out, and not for anything profound or mysterious in its construction but because it referred to me by a name I had not previously heard, and unlike the others I also sensed an element of humour in the way it was uttered. The name of course is 'Kismah' but at the time I did not understand its reference or meaning.

Eventually the voice stopped, and despite the occasional attempt to find some other connection with the statements I had heard and compare them with the changing aspects of my life or circumstance the whole period began to fade from memory.

Several years later my brother unexpectedly passed away. There was only eleven months between us and although we had once been close, in the years before he died our relationship had been quite difficult. As with most situations involving the loss of someone close I was left to regret the missed opportunity to remedy our situation. Inspired by the concept of self-analysis I embarked on a simple question and answer session in the hope that it would help me come to terms with my grief and the way I felt.

It was immediately after Christmas and with little else to occupy my thoughts during this particularly quiet period of my life I entered into the process with the expectation I would abandon it as soon as I allowed myself to be distracted by something else.

It took a while before I felt comfortable with the activity of examining my own thoughts but I soon got into a pattern and, as I had hoped, it slowly began to reveal a lot of memories and emotions I had long ago forgotten. I quickly started to immerse myself with the experience and the sessions began to last longer and longer as the hours would pass from one to the next without recollection of time or space. Like the magic that is often attributed to the simple action of questioning your thoughts, it helped to alleviate a lot of emotional sadness.

During these longer sessions I suddenly started to notice that the tone and subject of my dialogue would intermittently change, and I also began to find passages I had no memory or recollection of having written.

It was becoming quite frequent and started to encompass larger and larger sections of my writing, yet when I tried to deliberately observe or affect what was happening the passages became almost nonsensical and illegible. It was an unusual experience but there was something in the content of the material that intrigued me and I wanted to know more.

I concluded that the changes were occurring during particular states in my conscious awareness, but I didn't know or understand why it was happening. I would best describe it as being similar to the experience of arriving at a destination but not remembering having made the journey.

Whatever it was I was doing, or the way in which I was going about it had culminated in a pattern of intermittent trance. I was drifting in and out of conscious awareness, and when looking blankly at a piece of paper I soon discovered it was a relatively common occurrence.

Once I stopped trying to observe the process, the fluctuations that had previously made it difficult to understand what was being written had begun to disappear. It felt like I was on the periphery of a void attempting to dictate a slow stream of information, but then it began to speed up, and the faster I wrote it down the faster it came.

Sentence after sentence began to seamlessly flow from one to the next, as paragraphs quickly filled the pages without pause or hesitation. There were passages I did not immediately understand while others were very definite in their proclamations. After each session I would find myself reading them again and again in order to comprehend what it was saying or to construct a reply, but it seemed to instinctively know what that reply would be.

Before I could understand what was happening it turned into a marathon of questions and answers with no subject or query avoided, describing in detail almost everything from the simplest reaction in life to the effects of a dying star. Unknown worlds and civilisations, patterns of creation, who we are and where we are going and all with such simplicity and completeness I felt like I was standing on the edge of an ocean I never knew existed.

Days rolled into nights and the weeks into months, and if I wasn't writing then almost every waking thought was being consumed by this growing abundance of information but then, almost as unexpectedly as it began it suddenly stopped. I didn't want it to end, however it seems that it was a process and situation in which I had no choice. There was a promise that it would continue in another capacity at another time and left me with some questions of my own to consider, but as yet it has not returned, at least not in any way that I have noticed.

It was only when the main body of material was complete that the final scripted words made reference to the source of the material and an entity known as Kismah. It seems the voice of my past that had humorously whispered its name many years before had returned, yet no sooner had it ignited in me a thousand more questions, the opportunity to ask them had passed.

Although I cannot claim to fully understand the connection between us, it seems we are one and the same in that we have emerged from an identical strand of creation, however despite the attachment we are divided by two very different realities and he/she is more than one personality.

The passages in this book are the result of a communication between us, and with the exception of any grammatical corrections, it is a true and accurate documentation of the events as they occurred. These then are 'The Chronicles of Kismah,' providing us with an incredible insight into the extraordinary worlds in which we live.

The Original Question

Why do I feel bombarded with thoughts and in a majority of cases I don't seem to know where they come from?

They are the answers to your own questions, yet you do not recall them as such because you do not remember ever asking the question, just like you do not remember asking the question we are about to answer.

Why can I not remember asking it?

You are easily distracted by the emergence of other thoughts, and because you do not have the capacity to answer more than one at a time you layer one upon the other until eventually you forget having asked it.

Is that the reason why thoughts often come to mind spontaneously without any apparent reason?

Everything that you have wondered or been curious to understand does not disappear with the passage of another thought, but remains in place until an opportunity arrives in which it can be addressed. The only thing that separates a question from its answer is time, and in reference to time I am referring to a conscious construction, because in most cases the reaction and response is simultaneous.

I'm a little confused.

Then we must go back to the beginning and answer the question you had originally asked that precipitated this communication.

Which is?

Why do you accumulate so much emotion through the course of your life?

Did I actually ask that question or am I simply responding to an image that has been popping into my head for some time?

Now you have touched on the very thing upon which you are confused.

The question has originated from an answer I already have access to?

It is also a question that you have asked since you were a boy but it is only now that you have given yourself a moment to acknowledge the response.

Who exactly is it that responds?

As you have yourself just said, you responded to a question to which you already knew the answer.

So it is a bit of a chicken and egg situation?

We can see why it is you might think so, yet the truth is we placed it there in the hope that you would question it again. We thought it might be a more interesting strand with which to begin our communication as opposed to your thoughts regarding everything else.

I suppose you think I have been rambling?

On the contrary the translation of your thoughts prior to this communication has been most insightful, and a number of your assumptions are actually correct, but now you are finished we will attempt to enlighten you with the facts.

The facts regarding what?

The facts regarding everything you have a genuine desire to understand, and then maybe it will give you a little insight into the reason why we are reluctant to participate in the earth life system, unless of course we can be fairly confident it will bring us something we value.

Is this reluctance to participate the same for everyone?

For many they do not have the choice.

Why is this?

They have been a little less discerning in the manner in which they exposed themselves to the system without being aware of the implications.

I don't understand.

Then perhaps we should go back to the beginning and first try to explain the purpose of your own existence and this pattern of life on earth in which you are invariably lost.

I think it would help!

Then let us test your enthusiasm and hope that it matches up with our own and what we have to tell you. This system of life, or the focus of your current experience is imbued with certain limitations and restrictions, and although you cannot remember having made the choice, you were well aware of them before you came.

And why did I choose it?

For the same reason we choose anything, the challenge and the potentials it provides.

One of those challenges being that I wouldn't be able to remember having made the choice?

You can be certain that if it wasn't part of the original design then it is quite clear it has become one now.

Is that where the challenge lies, not being able to remember who we are?

It is one of many challenges that the system provides, and yet not the most difficult to contend with before you can relinquish your attachment to it. Now the reason for this is because the pattern in which you are focused and the direction it is taking you is interwoven and connected to so many other patterns it is very easy to lose yourself to the design. Therefore to complete the course, as it was intended at least, requires innumerable cycles of life, and yet even this is no guarantee you will succeed.

Is that because it is addictive?

In some respects it could be described that way, however it is a little more complicated, but if nothing else we are patient, and so we shall endeavour to enlighten you with the sum total of our patience. Now the decision to participate in this pattern of life is taken for various different reasons, yet the prime motivation, as it is with most patterns of creation, is the desire to grow. However the difficulty is, for this particular venture at least, it is not quite as straight forward as deciding to participate, and if you suddenly change your mind once it has begun it is not like you can simply get up and walk away.

Why not?

For the same reason that if you choose to swim an ocean and then decide when you are half way across that you have changed your mind. Now assuming you have no intention of drowning you will have to either continue in the original direction or turn back, but you cannot suddenly decide to stop swimming.

So once we have made the decision to begin then we have to continue until it is completed. Is this a requirement?

It is the effect of your involvement that holds you to complete what you have started. Now we do not expect you to fully comprehend the meaning of this statement, not immediately at least, but we will attempt to explain it in a way that will give you some understanding into the purpose of your existence. Your creation and your involvement in this pattern of life has evolved from something we have given you, and this attachment, or sponsorship if you prefer is not something we can easily let go. We have essentially set you on a path to fulfil your own potential, but we have an interest and we cannot leave you, even if we could we would not want to.

So we are essentially one and the same?

We began as one and the same with the cluster of energy from which we have both emerged, and although we still maintain that connection we are separated by two very different realities.

But I am free to make my own choices?

Yes, but you are not free to explore all the potentials that are available, not yet at least, and until you have awoken to this realisation then in many respects you could say that we are responsible for your well being.

Like a guardian?

In some respects we may be described as such, however we are much more in that we are essentially part of one another, and just as you would not leave your child until he is of an age to realise his own choices, we will not leave you until you have achieved a level of awareness to realise the choices that are available to you.

Is this life, or my participation in this life then my choice or yours?

Initially it began with ours, but everything that came afterwards is yours.

What about this particular life cycle, or this person I am now?

It was your choice. We helped you view the various probabilities and potentials it might provide, and we organised your entry and the specifics of location including family etc, but it was your choice.

So which was the life you initially chose for me, or the one upon which I first became conscious to my existence here on earth?

One that began a very long time ago, however you have changed much since, and your choices of direction, and the manner in which you emerge from each cycle rarely ceases to surprise us, but the fact remains you are still here, and therefore so are we. So to refine the original strand we were following, with regards to our reluctance to engage ourselves fully into the system, you may understand why it is that we do not take lightly the decision to participate, particularly if we cannot be sure it will bring us something of value.

What about those you say have little choice?

You could say they were a little over enthusiastic with their decision to engage with the pattern before they had allowed themselves a moment to consider the limitations, or the consequences of what was involved.

In what way have they been over enthusiastic?

They have sponsored more lives than they could effectively manage, or did not wait for the correct entry points. They are much more enlightened now, and they have grown a great deal from their involvement, as we have grown from yours, however they will wait longer for their creations to emerge from the cycle of participation.

Why do they not choose the correct entry points?

In a majority of cases their choices are limited because there is not enough time or places available, and now there is a possibility they will not be finished by the time the pattern of human endeavour is scheduled to complete its course.

Does that suggest we don't have very long?

You have at least another fifteen hundred years of history to contend with, so there is a little while before we must give any thought towards a contingency, for the moment at least.

Is that not enough?

It terms of your perception of time it might appear so, but when you take into account the fact that the human experience has existed in its current form for over one hundred thousand years it isn't quite as long as you think. However there is hope that certain events and the changes they may encourage over the next two hundred years will accelerate your progress.

What about the cluster of energy of which we are a part? Do we have enough time?

Fortunately we have been a little more discerning with our choices, but then our interests are not as varied.

Why does it take so long?

The pattern of life and the direction it takes attracts so many elements that with each cycle it becomes more and more difficult, and so you return again and again attracting more of the same.

When did the whole process begin? How did I get here?

Think of yourself as a ball of energy that we have created, and in the beginning you are imbued only with the seeds of your creation, a structure of parts that although they may hint at the making of a particular identity, it is not known if any one part will dominate, or in which direction it will flow. All that is known within this structure of energy is that it exists and there is a desire, even if it does not yet know how that desire will manifest. This is how it was for you in the beginning, and as an extension of what we are, you are imbued with the same desire that inspired us to give you life, just as we began from the inspiration and extension of something else that gave life to us and so forth. However, in order to help you understand the meaning of that desire and create your own potential we set you on a course that you now know as the human experience.

And not an easy one by your own admission?

Yet it is the only one you have ever known, and as is the nature of creation it had to begin with our own desire.

Which was to participate in the earth life system?

Yes, although more by our desire to understand it than to participate, however it is a necessary requirement, and the reason we do not take the decision lightly is that our interest is specific, but we shall explain this in more detail a little later. Now it is from this inherent desire of ours that you are motivated into action, but to seek out your own direction and your own fulfilment from which you will begin to grow. However it is this process and this pattern of life in which you grow that you also attract more and more elements of the system, and slowly you start to become more of the system than the part that motivates you.

You mean I become more human than my original energy form?

Not so much more human, but identified with the pattern of existence in which you are accumulating your experience.

Is that what is meant when it is often referred to as an illusion?

It is in your perception and the definition of your physical existence that is the illusion.

Then the obvious question is why does the illusion not end when we die?

Because essentially you are not aware of anything else, and if you cannot perceive anything differently then the status quo, or your attachments to that which you can perceive must be maintained.

So we keep coming back again and again attracting more of the system.

Now you may begin to understand why we say it is

difficult.

Difficult for whom?

For all of us! We do not expect you to fully understand, particularly since we are divided by two very different realities, but there is not one part of us or our creation that we are not aware. We feel your pain, we feel your suffering and at times you draw from us more than we are able to give, and we are pained by the fact that we cannot give it.

It sounds very complicated.

And in many respects it is, but it is not without benefits.

Does anyone ever actually emerge from the system?

Frequently, but there is a pattern, a sort of arc in which your awareness varies.

What do you mean by an arc?

There is a pattern that many follow in which you slowly fall into the illusion before you begin to awake and emerge the other side.

Is this pattern part of the design?

We are not quite sure, but it is something we have observed. It forms a primary element of our interests and this is a variable of the design that we have discovered.

Am I also a victim of this arc?

With you it is slightly different, something we would best describe as being more of a 'U' shaped pattern as opposed to an arc.

What does that mean, or how did that affect things?

You fell very quickly into the system like a stone that was dropped into a deep ravine and we started to concede that perhaps it was going to be a long process, but then you began to emerge almost the same way and as quickly as you fell.

Was there any particular reason for this?

We are unsure, and whatever the cause it appears to be one of the many variables in the system that we do not understand.

So there is no set pattern?

There is a pattern that many follow, but there are variables.

Are there many that follow a similar pattern in which they quickly fall only to emerge in the same fashion?

With those who tend to follow a similar trajectory it is often expected and with you it was not.

Why is it expected?

Those who quickly emerge are usually at a particularly advanced level in their progress whereas you are still quite young. You have given us much to ponder, in the most positive aspect of course, but your pattern is still not complete.

Will that affect my progress?

It is not that it will affect anything in particular, except there is a possibility you may fall back in again, which often shows itself in the reasons why you are still so easily distracted.

Is this usual?

Not particularly, but then few have fallen and emerged so quickly either, and as we have said, your course is still incomplete.

What do you mean when you say incomplete?

There are your attachments, those you have affected and touched by your presence, both positively and otherwise. It is a tapestry in which various elements are interwoven and connected to one another.

Is that a little bit like karma and everything you affect?

It is in relation to your attachments and those with whom you are bonded, but there is no error except in your perception, and you do not have to make good the affects of your action or reaction, unless of course you choose to do so.

But what exactly are our attachments?

They are all those things that are intrinsically entwined with your expression of life and the reason you keep on returning, because without your continuation you cannot complete the pattern.

When you talk about the pattern and its completion, are you referring to the individual element of each life we live?

We are referring to the culmination of everything you will derive from the entire experience. Your pattern is that which defines your existence and your individual part in the design.

Do we all have a particular part in the design?

Even the smallest screw plays its part in the workings of the machine, and as its designer will often tell you, the machine cannot work without it.

So if everything is connected and it is so difficult then how do we extricate ourselves from the system, or emerge on the other side?

You must play your part and finish what you have begun.

How do we do that?

By making peace with the parts that you have touched and those that you continue to attract.

It sounds like we have all been thrown into an ocean from which we will never escape.

That is because you are concentrated on the negatives without appreciation of its joys. These attachments, the parts, the people with whom you are associated and have been for much longer than you are aware, they are not a ball and chain around your foot in which you must try and extricate yourself, they are your heart and your emotion. They are the sum total of everything you are and the parts of everything you will become, because without them you could not have achieved a single strand of the pattern you have so far created.

And are these attachments we accumulate a part of us?

They are the parts of your experience that help to define who you are, just as you have helped to define them. Everything we create we do so by adding to what has already been created. Like the greatest minds and concepts, they do not simply originate from thin air or a lucid moment of inspiration, they are the additions to a pattern that had already existed before, yet without this pattern upon which they were able to add their part there would be nothing for them to create. If you were to compare the compositions of Bach and The Beatles you might think that perhaps they have originated from two different worlds, and in some respects they have, yet beneath the layers that have each been added since the time of Bach you will see quite clearly that one has originated from the other.

So this is your speciality, or the area you are interested?

To look beneath the patterns which have been added, and in so doing we are going further and further back to the beginnings of creation.

To the original design?

Yes, however even that is a design upon a design.

So essentially you are looking for the creator?

The designers, or those that created this system have long since finished with this pattern, and so we look for the seed, the beginning, the original pattern upon which all the others have been developed.

But if what you say is correct then that seed will have originated from a design that was also created by someone else?

Yes!

But how far does it go back?

We do not know, except to say that somewhere beneath the layers there is a strand that will eventually lead us through the aperture.

To God?

To other systems, other strands and other patterns. Anything else beyond this we cannot be sure.

Is this something we must all do?

It is different for everyone, however it is something we choose, and it forms a primary element of our interest and a pattern that we follow, although eventually we must all return.

Through the aperture?

To the beginning of our inception.

And could I return now?

You are too small, and then there are the parts of which you are made.

You mean the cluster of energy?

The parts you have accumulated on your own. When it is time you may come with us as a part of the whole, a completed pattern, or you may choose to join another. If not then you must create your own as we have created ours.

How would I do this?

Through the extension of what you are, by adding to the patterns and leaving more than you have taken. There is a process, but when you reach a certain level you will begin to understand why it is worth the effort.

And do I have a choice?

It is from your own desire to complete what you have started that is the reason you are obliged to return to the system.   The irony of course is that the more you accumulate the more difficult it becomes to extricate yourself from the system.

Is this perhaps why some choose to die in childhood?

Invariably they are often at an advanced stage in the process. They are almost complete and so they choose to leave before they begin to accumulate any new attachments.

But if they are at an advanced stage then why do they go to the trouble of returning?

To benefit those with whom they are already attached, and to help them in their progress so that they too can emerge. The action of those who leave before the onset of adulthood is often done out of love for those they have touched. There is a bond and they do not wish to continue their journey without them. It is not without drawbacks, and of course it is emotional for those it most affects, but there is always a reason, and one they feel is worth the effort.

What about those they leave behind? They are often so affected by their loss they rarely get over it.

They do eventually, when the cycle is complete and they are together once more.

From Chaos to Order

I cannot help but think this communication is somehow the result of unresolved issues and lots of thoughts turning around in my mind.

Then perhaps you should think of our response as being the order that has emerged from the chaos.

I think the way my mind works chaos is often a good way to describe it.

You have an enthusiasm to know things that are not so easy to understand. Even for us they are sometimes difficult, but then we are not limited by the same restrictions that are an inherent part of human perception.

Assuming we cannot escape those restrictions is it still possible to find peace of mind?

It is certainly possible, and there are some who would confess to finding it a relatively simple achievement, however, it is how long you can maintain it for that is the challenge.

How do we maintain it?

By simply turning your attention away from the issues that occupies your thoughts, but then there is the possibility you will also turn away from the elements that provide the greatest potential.

So if we wish to benefit from the experience of life then we have to accept the conflict that accompanies it?

It would be relatively simple to shield yourself from certain parts, however by turning away from the experiences that stimulate a response there is the possibility you will also remove yourself from the elements that will accelerate your growth.

With those elements being?

Your emotions and the way you react to them.

Is there any particular reaction or emotion that is valued?

They all have a value, however it is with those that are not so easily generated that the greatest attention is focused.

Such as?

The spontaneous reaction that invokes certain feelings of compassion and empathy, or the yearning to nurture and protect.

What about love?

You may assume it is our interpretation of such that we are referring.

Your interpretation? I don't understand.

Current definitions have the propensity to encompass a great deal more than we understand it; therefore we tend to avoid the term so that you will be less inclined to misinterpret its importance.

Is it important?

It is a primary element of the design.

And is there a consequence to how we respond to these particular forms of emotion?

Let us say it is how you generate and react to certain forms of emotion that your progress is measured.

What of the purpose to grow, to add to the pattern or to leave more than we have taken?

This is a basic requirement of all creation, and everything we know that expresses a conscious awareness of its surroundings adheres to this principal.

So what is the importance of compassion and empathy etc?

It is for these spontaneous reactions that this particular pattern of life was created, however it is out of choice that we participate and is not a requirement.

Now you've lost me!

All of creation follows the principal pattern to grow, and every other pattern is a derivative or an extension of this principal. Now those that designed the system you are participating in created it for this very purpose, however in their desire to add to the basic pattern they have acquired a particular interest. Just as we have developed a specific interest in the intricacies of certain patterns and designs, they have developed a specific interest of their own.

And for those who designed it that specific interest is emotion?

Not just any emotion.

You mean compassion, empathy etc?

They are important components, however there are other requirements.

Such as?

We can best describe it as a specific emotion that is generated from an inexplicable bonding of minds that often occurs through a shared experience involving the extremities of the system.

Are you referring to the element of survival that often occurs through things like war or an experience that involves the threat of life?

Survival and the variety of ways it shows itself is a major factor, however it is in the sharing of the experience and the union it engenders between two people that the emotion is expressed.

So it is essentially the expression of love?

It may be described as such, but not as you have come to understand it.

Can we express the same type of emotion from an ordinary relationship between two people who are in love?

If the union is of a particular intensity and it has been prolonged to form a dependency then it is possible, but alone it is not enough nor is it a guarantee. In most instances a long relationship is usually the prelude to a cycle of union in which they will go on to share many different roles, or it is a symbol of one that is coming to an end. The fact is, no one fully understands why it is generated other than to say it is a spontaneous reaction to the system of survival, and in its natural form it is extremely rare. So rare even that it is possible you may live through the experience of numerous different cycles without ever generating it.

So can I assume that I am not a great contributor of this emotion?

There has been a moment when you were exposed to its potentials, but it is still in progress. Think of it as a scattering of white buttercups in a field of barley.

Which doesn't sound like very much.

And sometimes that is all it requires, although like we have said, in its natural form it is extremely rare, but valuable to those who value it.

Do you value it?

We have grown much from our exposure, and there are many other patterns that produce it in various degrees of intensity, but it does not form the basis for our particular interest nor is it the reason why we participate. Our primary interest is the design and the various patterns that grow from it, although in comparison to the majority that participate we are relatively small.

In what way do mean you are small?

We can be likened to a group of surveyors in a small office on the periphery of a large city complex. No one really knows that we are here, and even if they do they have little reason to be concerned by our presence and so let us go about our business undisturbed. We take measurements and calculations that require us to visit certain districts, and for the duration it takes us to survey a particular area we are its residents. Yet unlike the locals who live and breathe each pattern of the environment, playing out different roles and adding to the various patterns they are immersed, we only play a small part.

Until you have all the information you need?

In a manner of speaking yes, however in this system where so much emotion is generated before you can produce any that is valued, you must follow a particular path and therefore it is not as straightforward as simply going in and coming back out again.

Do you have to follow a particular course and direction?

Yes, and in this pattern of activity that you know as the human experience, it is a lengthy process, and in a majority of cases we lose more than we can retrieve.

What do you mean when you say you lose?

We lose them to the system; however not in the sense that we cannot find them, but that they lose themselves to the design in such a way they forget who they are, a little bit like you have.

Even though I realise it is not real?

But you are still lost to the system as you cannot perceive anything beyond it, and even if you could there is no guarantee that you will not fall back in and lose yourself all over again, not to mention your attachments.

So it isn't like you will lose them forever?

We certainly hope not, yet we still wait for some to return.

And when do you expect this to happen?

When they are finished and they are ready to relinquish the attachments that holds them to believe there is more in the experience than it can actually provide.

How can you help them?

The same way that we have helped you, by waiting until they are of a mind to question the validity of their experience, or when it no longer provides them with the opportunity to fulfil their potential.

And if that doesn't work?

Then we wait.

Is there nothing you can do?

It is their choice and while they see value in the experience there is little anyone can do that will make them see it differently, but there is a pattern and many follow a similar direction until eventually it no longer captures their imagination. Our best chance is when one begins to emerge who is bonded to another, and if they are also bonded to someone else and they in turn to another then the potential is magnified.

Why is it your best chance?

Because it is highly unlikely that someone who has begun to emerge from the illusion will want to leave the system while those with whom they have bonded are still a part of it.

So essentially the only way of extracting yourself from the pattern is through an emotional attachment?

As we have been saying, it is all part of the design.

Is this what is meant when they say it is all about love?

Yes, but not just any kind of love, or one that is easily generated.

Except through an event of extreme circumstance?

In most instances this is only the beginning and it will still require the activity of many more cycles before any noticeable effect begins to galvanise a union of minds.

Is it important that we play different roles?

It is not a requirement, although it is a pattern of integration that many will choose.

Is this because we will react differently to one another depending on the roles we take?

It is chosen by way of experiencing one another through the interaction and accomplishment of a shared goal.

Is this how many cycles begin, with the purpose of achieving a specific goal?

In some instances yes, but you will still have many things to work out alone. It is a completely individual process and there are no rules.

If we had completed our course but were to continue with the cycles of life in order to help someone else emerge is there a danger we would form new attachments and fall back in even further?

It happens frequently, however once they begin to emerge and wake to the realisation that they are in a dream it is very rare they will fall back in completely as it was when they first began, and at this stage they are often very particular about the cycles they choose.

Is this the result of those who experience an early death in order to reduce the possibility of creating new lasting attachments?

In some instances yes, and they are often much older than their years suggest.

And their bond, or their attachment is with their parents?

In most cases it will be either one or both parents, but it may also be a grandparent, a brother or a sister, or it might even be a friend, but usually it is with those who are most affected by their departure.

Divided Realities

What is reality like for you compared to me?

It is very much like your reality but with greater variety and less restriction.

And what form do you take?

It depends on the circumstances of our activity, but in a majority of cases we will take on various forms that we have experienced from previous areas of existence, and yet at other times we may take on something completely new. You could say that we are only restricted by our imagination.

Do you experience the same sensations of touch and taste etc?

Yes, however we are not limited by the human scope of sense and perception, and so therefore we have the propensity to experience them all and many more you are unaware of. When you look upon a field of poppies you perceive them as being similarly identified yet we sense the differences and variations including those of the environment from which they have each emerged. From their colour there is a taste and in their texture there is a sound, but with the restrictions placed upon your conscious sensitivity you are currently unaware of these.

And are there fields of poppies where you are?

Like you cannot imagine.

But who creates these fields, or the environment in which you experience them?

We do.

How do you do this?

We bring them with us, as you will bring yours with you, and we will share in them, to wander through the fields as you have wandered, to feel the joys you have experienced, and in turn you will explore the worlds that we have explored.

Are there no limits?

We have in our cluster the environments of entire planets including many of the life forms they sheltered, and it is constantly growing, yet even though you are not aware of them you have already added many of your own.

So in your world, your reality is made up of what you have personally experienced?

Essentially yes, however we still maintain the potential to create with our imagination, and we have explored many worlds that we have had neither experience of nor influence in, but we can still imagine what it might have been if we had.

I don't understand?

There are many worlds and civilisations that are no longer a part of any evolving design or system, but they are still alive to those who have a mind of curiosity to explore them. And even though you cannot influence or play any part in what they have been it does not lessen in value the potentials it once provided for those who had helped to create them.

Are there many of these worlds and civilisations that are no longer a part of an evolving design?

More than you might imagine, and some that are quite elaborate in that they would take the equivalent of many lifetimes to explore, while some are simple constructs leaving only the basic remnants and information in reference to those who created them.

Is there a reason why they were created?

They were designed for various different purposes such as recreation or to replicate and mirror the environments in which they were participating. However the most elaborate are those created by previous civilisations for the purpose of leaving behind a record detailing their course and history. It is in these that we are most interested.

It all sounds fascinating?

And the reason why we frequently lose ourselves to their designs, yet it can be frustrating for us also, because even the most detailed environments lack the finer threads that help us to fully comprehend the various layers and patterns of endeavour. The reality is that without some form of participation it is almost impossible to fully understand them, which is made more difficult by the fact that they no longer exist.

In what sort of detail can you explore these other environments?

It depends on what they have left behind, but in most instances we can explore certain moments in their history, various buildings and structures including their cities and landscapes. In some cases we can even see the world they had created through their own eyes and feel some of the emotions they had experienced.

But if you can explore all of this then why is it so frustrating?

Because it is only a replication and there is no potential to either act or respond.

Is this important?

Without reaction it is difficult to fully appreciate or understand the pattern they have created.

And you cannot change anything?

There is nothing we wish to change, we only desire to experience, and without the potential to act and respond to that experience we are limited, just like someone who might like to explore a two dimensional painting. The picture may tell you a lot about the perception of its creator, about his strokes and his technique or what he was trying to portray, whether he had succeeded in doing so or not, but it can never tell you anything about the artist, because the truth is that without him it will only ever be a reflection. It is the same for those who choose to explore the probabilities of a previous cycle, because no matter how they may view the various directions they could have taken instead there is little they can do to change or alter what it is.

But would you want to change anything?

When you can clearly see that a certain action or reaction could have altered the whole shape and direction of a particular event that you are no longer able to affect then you will understand why it is a difficult undertaking.

Surely the potential to re-experience the joyous moments of our lives is something many people would cherish.

Yes, and there are many who choose this direction for that very reason, but when you are coming towards the end in relation to your cycles of participation there is a danger it will also entice you with potentials that are no longer available.

Is that because they are gone, and so therefore they can never be recreated to produce the same experience?

The potentials are no longer available because you are no longer the person who experienced it. You have changed and you are more, and despite the joys of experiences past, there is only the desire to change and be more again. It is for this reason that in your attempt to add another layer and come alive to its potential it may require that you forget who you are in preparation for what you will become.

But if we can forget who we were, temporarily or otherwise, then why can we not experience it all again just like looking through the eyes of a child?

You may forget but you are still changed, and so therefore everything else around you will also be changed. When you observe a child as she plays she may be ignorant to anything that she has experienced before, and be surprised by the seeming newness of things that have already been seen, but she is changed and so will it be for the environment she is experiencing. It matters little how much we are immersed in the light of our endeavour, whether we have a memory of it or not, but we cannot help but grow, even if we are not aware of how we have been affected.

Then what you are saying is in these worlds that have gone before you cannot grow?

Not in a way that has any significant affect. They are interesting and we are touched by the experience, but there is nothing more than what they have left for us to observe, and so in relation to our own desire and intention they are dead.

How are they dead?

They are complete, and we cannot grow from a world that is complete, and even the patterns that invite us to explore them further are also dead because we cannot see beneath the layers to utilise or understand how they were completed.

So a perfect world is a dead world?

If it is complete and you cannot add to it or grow then what else can it be?

So when you say you will wait, it is not like you don't have anything to do?

On the contrary we have more than we are able to contend with.

It sounds like your existence is simply a maze of exploration.

And like a maze it is also possible to lose yourself in the design, and for very long periods.

In what way do you mean lose yourself?

Just like you have lost yourself to the system in which you are currently participating, only in these completed worlds we maintain at all times a conscious awareness of our reality, and there is little of the limitation or restrictions that you are acquainted with.

So you cannot lose yourself in a way that I am lost in this one?

It is only in our interest that we are lost, a little like an architect who might discover a building he has never seen before. Once inside it could be many hours before you see him again, but in the exploration of these other patterns it can be much longer?

How long?

It varies on the complexity and the detail left behind by those who created them, but in some instances it can be equivalent to many years, while for others it may be centuries.

Centuries?

Metaphorically speaking of course! Time here is a very different concept than it is for you there, but we shall talk about this at another point.

Regardless of how you experience the movement of time, to lose yourself for centuries to a system you have yourself labelled a dead world is a very long period.

And how long do you think we have been involved with this one that is still very much alive?

I don't know!

There is over a thousand years in your life alone, and there are more we have yet to retrieve, not to mention the numerous completed forms that make up our cluster.

That sounds like a lot of experience?

As I have said, we are very small in comparison to most, but like you we are easily distracted.

But how much detail and information from this system can you possibly need?

How much have you retrieved from this life alone?

I don't know, but it seems like a lot.

Try and imagine once more the scattering of white buttercups in a field of barley.
When you put it that way I suppose it doesn't sound like very much.

And yet it is still valuable, and even more so now that you have begun to emerge.

Am I emerging?

You would not be capable of this translation if you weren't.

And when we have all completed the course, will we too be able to explore these other worlds?

If that is what you choose then the option will be available, but for now it would benefit you more if you were to finish what you have begun.

Is it not possible to explore these other systems between each cycle of existence?

It is possible and in some instances we have endeavoured to show you some, but you are impatient and there are many aspects that you would not be able to understand. There is also a danger it may affect your goal and purpose here. As we have said you are easily distracted so the distraction of another world that offers little potential might not be an option you would want to choose, remembering of course that completion is the key.

I cannot help being curious, and the idea of exploring these other worlds ignites my imagination.

As they have a propensity to ignite ours. When it is time and you are receptive to the experience we shall endeavour to show and bring to life the wanderings of your imagination, and we are sure you will not be disappointed. In the meantime it would be best if you were to concentrate on that which your imagination has not yet completed.

And when will it be completed?

When it is no longer capable of holding your awareness and you have relinquished your attachments.

What about these other worlds, the patterns and their environments? How will I know when you are showing me?

You will know because they will be like nothing we have shown you before, and in this we shall hold your curiosity, but for now we must finish with this pattern in which your curiosity has yet to be satisfied.

Drugs and Addiction

Will we ever see the people we once knew in this life who have since passed away?

The fact is you see them all the time, but such are the limitations in your conscious awareness many do not often recall the experience.

Sometimes I dream about people who have passed away. I cannot help feel that is not really a valid experience, at least not in the sense of an everyday encounter in which I remembered them.

That is because you now reside in two very different worlds, however there is no one who is ever lost to you, even though this is how it appears. If you knew them in life then you will know them again.

You mean when we too have passed away?

When you have transferred your own focus of awareness towards their reality, but you will not see it while you are focused on another.

Is it possible we will we share a similar relationship?

It will depend on the moments you have already shared

and the level of attachment. If there is no other cycle in which you have shared a previous relationship then it is likely to continue very much as you had experienced prior to their departure, however it is only natural that the change in circumstance will also generate a change in the relationship.

Is that simply because we will no longer be participating in the system?

And also because you will have both been changed by the experience.

My brother died recently, when I see him again will it still seem like we are brothers?

It is unlikely, because in the circumstances that you are referring to it will be quite clear that you are not.

In the circumstances I am referring to?

In the knowledge that the basis of your relationship was only a part you were obliged to play. It is quite possible you may know each other from another role you have experienced in another time and place, and in some instances you will revert instantly to other characteristics of a different relationship. It will simply depend on who you were before the most recent cycle.

So it is possible we may not even look like one another?

We are fairly certain that you won't.

How can you be so sure? Perhaps being who we were in this life is the only common ground we will share.

We can be sure because we are in a position to know that this is not the case, and if all you have is that which you have shared from this particular cycle then there would be very little to preserve.

It wasn't an easy relationship?

That is because you both chose two very different courses. However you have more in common than you suppose, yet there were difficulties that had to be addressed and you had little patience in trying to overcome them.

We were different and sometimes I feel that I should have been a little more understanding?

You had your own course and direction to contend with, and even if you had managed to understand him better it would have made little difference to his choices and the direction that he chose. What may surprise you is that his life was far more successful than you have imagined.

Even though he probably died as a result of his addiction to drugs?

He died because he had finished his course. Whether the completion of that course came through the addiction to drugs or an accident makes little difference, other than to say that his moment had come.

How was it successful?

How was it not?

Maybe because of the way he had hurt people and the type of life he had led.

They were only hurt because he did not exist in a way they were willing to understand. We accept this is not how it might appear, but there were many who grew more from his experience than he grew from theirs. The difficulty of course is that for those around him they could only see a sequence of disaster and self-destruction; yet it may surprise you to know that in this chaos there was in fact order. You did not see it because you could only see what you had allowed yourself to understand, but he was more content than you realised. He lived a life that he chose and we can tell that in his part he is more than happy.

What about now that it's over?

He has much to reflect on and it may take a number of cycles before he fully recovers from his experience, but he will emerge from it a greater being.

Where is he at this moment?

In an environment not dissimilar to the one in which he existed in this cycle.

I often dream about him, and I tend to see him very much as I remember him, but the place he seems to reside does not resemble what you might call a heavenly environment.

And yet this is what he chooses because it reflects his attachments and he maintains a desire to nurture them. There are patterns that offer him enormous potential for growth and so he will spend time in its environment until he knows best how he can exploit them.

How long will he spend in this environment?

It will depend, however he will use it like a springboard to explore various strands of the tapestry he is creating.

What do you mean by a springboard?

One in which he will go on to explore what he has created through various other cycles of existence.

Will I share in any of those other future cycles?

It is possible, however you have accumulated stronger attachments elsewhere, and it is highly likely these will form the focus of your awareness for some time.

I find that very sad.

We cannot explore every strand of the tapestry in which we are involved, and even if it were possible it would take too long to complete.

Did he specifically choose the life he has just led?

He chose certain strands of it, and the rest were simply the probabilities of his existence. You played your part in these probabilities, but there were others whose part was greater.

I still don't understand what his life had achieved. He was addicted to drugs for much of his adult life so surely he must have created a trail of hurt and regret that he will want to put right.

You do not see it now but the majority of those loose ends that you have assumed he had left unattended he put right before his departure, and as we have said, his life was more of a success than you have guessed.

And is there any regret?

There is always regret. Even for those who have lived the most fulfilling life there is still an element of regret. If however you are asking is there any form of atonement or recompense for either his actions or reaction in life then you must understand this is not how it unfolds. Many will have regrets and if they are brave enough to go on and explore the various probabilities and choices that could have changed certain aspects of their course and direction then they may have more than they wished, but there is no atonement. If one is to die as a result of an addiction it does not in any way suggest their life was unfulfilled, and in a majority of cases there will be many associated with their predicament that will have grown from the experience.

If you were to look at someone whose life has been affected by addiction it is not always so easy to see it?

That is because for the most part you do not see it. The fact remains it is their world and one that they have created.

What about the cluster or group they are part of? Does it have any bearing on why someone might be inclined to follow a particular course and direction involving addiction?

In relation to many lives that might be inclined to follow a pattern of physical addiction they are often very different in that their interests are focused on areas we would prefer to avoid. Invariably they grow from patterns we consider to be extreme, and not because they are any less fulfilling, but they tend to be more testing and require greater involvement and participation than we are willing to invest. We share different interests and purposes, and in relation to any previous involvement we know little about them, although in the case of your brother we have learnt more from your involvement.

I cannot help but think that in cases involving addiction and those who are invariably affected by their actions the attachment between them isn't very strong?

There is no one you have encountered positively or otherwise that does not touch or change in some way your own course and direction. Unfortunately in many cases involving those who succumb to addiction their touch is often greater than many are willing to accept or are able to remember.

Is that because in the type of life they lead it prevents us from understanding them?

In some respects yes. In relation to your brother and those who shared a similar life on the streets they had little difficulty understanding him and often referred to him as the professor. He knew about things they were not aware of until he came into their world. They were surprised by the fact he had relinquished something they coveted, yet he chose a lifestyle like theirs in which they thought they had not been given a choice. They had accepted him as their own because in many ways they were one and the same, but there was a difference, and they were aware of it. Many of those he met on the streets believed they had an excuse, and a reason for being who they were, but for your brother it was a choice. It was a choice for them also but they did not see it that way. They shared the drugs and the experience this provided but there was always a difference, and nowhere was this more evident than when he played his music. Hence the reason why they referred to him as the professor. In this life he managed to reach a place that for the most part is alien to you, and he changed people you could not have changed in a dozen cycles, unless you could appear to them as an image they would identify. In this then they identified with him perfectly. He was different in their world and they had accepted him because in theirs he had accepted them.

Is it true that when someone chooses this particular path they hurt a lot of people in the process, yet we all feel helpless because often there is very little we can do about it?

The earth life system is an extreme pattern of existence so it is expected that many of the reactions from those who are exposed to it will also be extreme. They are hurt not by someone's choice or the path it may have taken them but by their own reaction to it. The difficulty involving cases when it appears someone has not lived up to their potential is there are many with whom they are attached who think perhaps they are somehow responsible. The fact remains it is not your choice and so therefore there is very little you can do that will change it.

But can another person's course, and particularly their choices potentially affect both the course and choices of someone else?

You choose your own course and you also choose how you will respond to the courses of others. Your brother has lived, and for those who were connected to him through his choices they too have lived because of them.

In what way have they lived?

In the way he has enhanced their perception and opened their eyes to another world. In many respects he made his life difficult, yet no one drove him to drugs. He chose them simply because he enjoyed how they made him feel, and he pursued them, including the various experiences they promised, very much in the same way you pursue your own enjoyment. He was happy in his world, and unlike those who profess to be happy in theirs, he slept easily. His difficulty now is that his happiness was derived from an attachment he cannot take with him, and it may take a while before he will learn to live without them again.

You mean the drugs?

It was not so much the drugs but the patterns that revolved around them. They were a means to a particular goal and purpose, but now he may pay a price many would not be willing to sacrifice.

In what way will he pay a price?

He will have to examine the intricacies of what he has created in order to extract the elements he values and explore them. Without this the pattern he has created will always require an element he cannot take with him.

With regard to his pattern, are you talking about his life?

We are talking about the pattern of fulfilment and the various elements that he will value from the experience.

The attachments he cannot take with him, are you referring to the drugs?

We are referring to all the addictions he must relinquish. It is the same for all who participate in the system, and not only with reference to physical dependency, yet for him and those who are addicted to particular substances the challenge is often greater.

So do we all have addictions?

In various degrees of intensity there are very few alive today who are not part of the system because of some form of dependency or addiction.

In what way are we addicted?

In every element that you covet the experience of life! Ask of yourself what it is that you are unwilling to relinquish in life and then know that is your addiction and the reason it is you are here. These are your challenges and what you must eventually relinquish before you can extract yourself from the pattern.

So then what you are saying is that the greater our addiction to life then the greater the challenge?

In a manner of speaking, yes, however some challenges are more difficult than others.

And is an addiction to either drugs or similar substances the most difficult?

It depends on what the pattern of life derives from the attachment. It is different for everyone. Some are able let go without a second thought, but usually this is because they do not see any value in holding onto the attachment. However for your brother this is not the case because he has placed a value in the pattern that his dependency has helped to produce.

What is he doing at this moment?

He is living out the structure of his experience, as he would like to have lived it on earth.

How long will he spend doing this?

It is difficult to say but there is interest in what he has produced so we expect it may be some time.

Some time before what?

Before he returns to the cycle of participation. He has much to explore and his attachments may prove challenging, but like we say there is interest.

Why is there interest?

Because he has derived an element of fulfilment, which

has been generated from a particular strand.

Are you referring to an element of value that he placed on the experience?

In essence, yes, but for those who follow a similar course involving drugs it is different. They see the experience through the eyes of someone with a distorted perception that creates a difference and an intensity that is rarely found elsewhere.

Are you referring to the intensity created through taking drugs?

We are referring to the extremities of emotion that he has generated from his dependency. There is little to be gained from the experience a particular substance might help to produce. It may appear that the drugs are helping you to feel a certain way, or to see things that you were previously unclear, but in a majority of cases this is only an illusion.

Yet some people believe that certain drugs help them to experience a reality others cannot see, and in some cases it is this that creates the addiction.

It may help them to experience a distorted version of a reality that they do not understand, but in most instances the drugs are simply helping to override a set of filters that were put into place for a reason.

Which is?

To focus on the experience in which you are participating. To perceive anything more, or to look beneath the surface of your existence towards the greater part of reality that is its motivation will simply negate the challenges you have chosen. You are either in the game or you are not. You see the reality as it was designed or you see the patterns upon which it is being designed.

Can anyone or anything exist in both worlds?

Only those who have designed it, and you are not of that level nor are we, including many of those who choose to participate. There are some who are proficient in the manipulation of the energy field upon which the expression of life depends, but they have little interest in this system or any other similar pattern.

Why are they not interested?

They do not feel it is worth the effort, or there is little potential to be found in its limitations, yet even they cannot exist in two worlds at once. You are either the driver or the mechanic, and if you are curious to see under the bonnet then you cannot do it while you are driving the car. You can try, and for a moment it may appear that you have succeeded, but ultimately it will only hasten your exit from the game.

Is there a reason for this?

You are limited in your capacity to perceive the reality of what you are, and it is the same for those who are immersed in the structure of science and the elements you refer to as Quantum Physics. They are attempting to find order in a structure they do not have the capacity to understand, and the reason for this is because they are limited. They are simply trying to wrap a picture of their own restricted reality around a structure that is unlimited, and so no matter how great their perception or their endeavour to understand, the picture cannot fit. Not that this will in anyway dampen their enthusiasm, but there is many a great scientist who has lost his mind in the attempt, just like those who have taken drugs in the hope they can bypass a filter system that was designed to prevent it. If there is an answer that you seek then it is in the reality of the world you wake up to each morning with a mind that is open to its potential that you will find it, not in a world that either intoxicates or blinds you to it. Whereas a drug addict has blinded himself to the drugs, your scientists and physicists blind themselves with the curiosity of their ego.

Surely that's not the same as someone who takes drugs?

Give a man the experience of any drug he can consume and that which he can produce himself in the light of recognition and applause and then ask him which he would prefer. Whether you accept it or not, the fact remains you are in the game, and for a reason you have chosen. If you wanted to be a part of the reality that underlies it then you can be certain you would have chosen this instead.

So taking drugs or going down any route that might promise you an insight into the reality that underpins our existence is not something that will benefit us?

Unless of course you have acquired a particular level of awareness in which you will understand it, yet it is highly unlikely that anyone in such a position would ever be tempted to follow this direction. You can be sure they already know what exists beyond their perception, but they have chosen to participate instead.

Is this why it often appeared he had lost control of the real world?

He had begun to lose control of the illusion because he had seen hints of his reality, which he could not affect.

Was that through drugs?

His filters were greatly impaired. When he finally tried to live without his attachments and change his direction it was too late. His world had changed and so had the one he attempted to pursue in its place.

He had seen beyond the veil?

He had seen only a shimmering beyond the veil, but it was enough and he was greatly changed by it, as are those who are tempted to follow a similar course. Despite how it might often appear to the observer, it is rarely the drugs that kill them.

Is this the same for everything we choose to indulge in?

Take in what you will if it brings you joy, just be sure you can let it go when it is finished.

And when will we know it is finished?

When it fails to bring you joy.

I cannot help but think that there was maybe something more I could have done.

He made his choices as you have made yours. You have shared a moment and you are both the greater for having done so, and you will meet again of this we are sure.

Will we ever share another life?

If that is what you both choose then there is every reason to expect it will happen, and even if you choose not to, there will still be many moments and opportunities in which to share another experience. The truth is you have been doing so since his departure, you simply do not recall the adventure, but we assure you that in his new world you are not a stranger.

Is that the place I recall as not being too dissimilar to the world he left behind?

That is what he chooses, and it is an environment he is most comfortable. He is content that his course is complete, and despite any contrary opinion it is for you he is most concerned, because you have yet to finish yours.

Life between Life

Will most of us return to surroundings similar to those we experience here on earth after we die?

It depends on the individual and the details of the life they have just completed, but for most they will often return to an environment that is familiar, at least until they have had time to readjust.

Who creates these places we go to afterwards?

They are the culmination of various cultures and life experiences that have been generated over many thousands of years.

So they appeal to most cultures and life experiences?

If not then they can add to them or make alterations as they prefer.

Is that possible?

You are only restricted by your imagination.

Can you create an entirely new environment?

If you have a particular desire or inclination to do so, but generally it is rare and only pursued by those who have completed their course and attained a particular level of awareness.

I have often thought that during sleep we visit people who have passed away?

It happens frequently, even though many do not recall the experience, but often that is because there is a large part of their reality they are not aware of.   The interaction between the two realities is usually more common soon after one has passed over and during a period of readjustment until they are ready to move on.

Where exactly do they go?

Many will go on to prepare for the next cycle while some will return to their cluster.

And after they have readjusted to their new environment is there still interaction?

Yes, but it will be of their own choosing and less frequent.

Why is this?

They have much to work out and they do not wish to be distracted, particularly if that distraction is an attachment from a previous cycle because then there is the potential it will have an influence on their choices. If there is a bond that has been created over numerous different cycles, and it is one with which they intend to continue their association, then interaction may be more frequent.

What about interaction between two people who have both passed away?

It will be the same as if one were still alive, except they would both maintain a recollection of the event.

Would there be much interaction between say my mother and my brother who are both deceased?

She is a regular visitor to his new environment.

And what is the basis of their relationship?

It is not too dissimilar to the one they shared on earth. She gives him advice on certain issues and he still chooses not to take it. He is content and does not appear to be in any rush to change his situation.

The strangest thing is that since my brother died I seem to recall many dreams in which we share certain moments in a particular place, yet I can never recall sharing any with my mother?

With your mother it was different. There was a period of readjustment but it was very short, and although a line of communication was maintained between those with whom she had been attached, the emotion was often too strong to hold it for any length.

Is there a particular reason for this?

The entire cycle had been a huge emotional experience with those she had been closely associated and she needed time alone to evaluate the pattern. There were difficulties she had not accounted for, and certain probabilities had not quite played out as she had hoped.

In what way were there difficulties?

The suicide of her father was an element that affected her course.

Does that mean it wasn't part of any plan?

Suicide is rarely part of anyone's plan but it happens, and those who are most affected by it must deal with the situation as best they can in the hope that it does not alter too greatly their course and direction, including the choices they had made or will have to make because of it.

Did this greatly affect my mother?

It affected the course and direction of an entire group, as is nearly always the case. It is merely one of the many variables in the system you have to contend with. She did better than expected, but she was particularly hard on herself and thought she could have dealt with it differently.

Is this why she needed time alone?

You all need time alone to evaluate the completion of each cycle, only sometimes the effect of participating in the pattern of life on earth requires a little longer than others, which is often made worse by the fact that you have no memory of who you are while you are a part of the system. Prior to this cycle she had reached quite a level of perception, however she took on a greater role than she had anticipated, or given herself time to prepare, and her ability was not quite at the level required for the situation she encountered. Like I have said she did better than expected but she felt that she could have done more.

In the few recollections that I have of her in my dreams she often appears to be quite serious and aloof.

She is wary of creating too many situations from her existing attachments that may inspire another new direction of participation, at least not until she has given herself time to explore the various options available from what she has already created. She is also aware of certain intricacies involving your own cycle and she does not wish to interfere with the process.

What do you mean when you say she had reached quite a level of perception?

She perceived the loneliness that enticed the awakening of her compassion. It is a rare occurrence in the human endeavour and therefore requires a specific level of detail and precision in order to nurture and preserve its potential.

It's potential for what?

To transform and be transformed!

Is this the same as what you were saying earlier in relation to generating a specific emotion?

Yes, but in certain individuals their compassion, or the emotions surrounding it is ignited without the extremities that is often a major ingredient. No one quite knows where it comes from or why it occurs, and so there is interest.

Are we not all imbued with some form of compassion?

Only when it is brought to your attention, and even then it is contrived. It is a natural reaction to the system you are exposed to and is generated in its purest form from those with whom it emerges spontaneously and without thought to its consequence.

I assume it is not something that I have a propensity for?

Only what you have experienced by association. Like we say in its natural form it is extremely rare.

Even in a system that was designed to express it?

Particularly so, because if nothing more it brings to our awareness just how rare it is.

I find it difficult to understand why there is so much interest when it seems to be such a natural expression of life, but then like you say I grew up with it.

There were others from the same cluster that shared in her cycle by relation and so you were more exposed than would have normally been the case.

So I am also guessing that we have not emerged from the same cluster or group?

I think you know this already, and for all that we admire about her cluster and their skills of perception, the ability to survive the extremities of the earth life system at the expense of another isn't one of them.

You are referring to me?

In the most complimentary manner of course!

The ability to survive at the expense of someone else doesn't sound like much of a compliment.

And yet it is more of one than you think, and it is an ability that sits perfectly beside the goals and aspirations that you have set out to achieve, however your exposure to someone else's ability has helped you to develop in other areas which has the potential to benefit your progress.

Does this imply that by nature I am not a compassionate individual?

By nature you are an observer and translator of design, and by nature she was a perceiver of effects. You grow from interaction and the sharing of differences. Just as you have grown from your exposure to her perception, she has grown from her exposure to your observation. It is the same for all interaction, and even the smallest that adds to the pattern brings something of value.

Is this why there can sometimes appear to be huge differences between the various personalities of a family unit?

Invariably each has something that the other does not, and through various modes of interaction and exposure you attach a little bit of what the other has to yourselves. It is an element of the design that helps to accelerate your growth and progress through the tapestry of creation in which we are all a part.

When you said that there were others that came together from the same cluster, is this common?

On the contrary it is rare. It is usual to participate with those whom you have bonded from a previous cycle or attachment but not from the same cluster.

Is there a particular reason or purpose for doing this?

Often those that choose to enter the system as a group are attempting to achieve a specific goal with the intention of providing a variable, or a seed of alteration.

Did they succeed?

It is too early in the process to tell, and it may take hundreds of years before there is any noticeable effect, or it may not take any effect at all. It is merely a ripple in the ocean and as yet no one really knows in which direction it will flow.

How many came together from the same group?

There were four of them. One is still alive and the other died young, although it was not intended for her to live as long as she did.

Why was this?

Their plan had been compromised with the suicide of your grandfather. It was anticipated that she would have completed her cycle much sooner, however for reasons you are aware it was delayed.

I remember her. She was newly married and she could not have children.

She was never meant to live long enough to have been given the choice, nor was it her intention to have entered into a union of marriage. As we have said, her situation had been compromised and so therefore her cycle was extended.

Was it part of the design or her plan not to have children?

It was part of the design not to create any new attachments. She was at a very advanced stage in her progress and she did not wish to create anything more that would require further cycles and prolong her participation. Her role had been generated with the intention of helping the others in her group, and her death was to be the impetus for the completion of a particular goal.

Is this the same for most early deaths?

For some yes, for others it is either a lack of desire to assimilate themselves to the cycle and its environment, or something has changed that prevents them from achieving a specific goal. In the majority of cases where it has been planned it is often intended as a challenge for those who are closely associated with them and for the purpose of accelerating their growth in a particular area.

Did they complete their goal as they had intended?

It is still in progress; although it is the generations that follow them will they know if they have succeeded.

Will they return?

Yes but not for some time, or in this particular era of change and evolution.

What about the one who died young?

She will return for one last cycle and, provided she does not generate any new attachments, her participation in the earth life cycle will be complete.

And what of any of the new attachments she has created from this life?

She will see them out in another environment.   To complete them through the cycles of participation will only tempt her back into other sequences of experience she has already completed.

Could that not also happen when she returns for her last cycle?

She will choose a sedentary existence with little exposure to the emotional elements that you are most familiar with.

But even though they are at an advanced stage in their progress they can still be tempted back in?

It is possible and it happens, but usually when they attain a certain level of awareness the potentials to do so are diminished.   In circumstances involving a cycle that precipitates your completion you will choose your part carefully and plan for any eventualities.

I would have thought we all choose our parts carefully.

It depends on what you hope to gain from the experience, however opportunities are limited and many are impatient. They will grow from whichever course and direction they choose but they would grow much quicker if they waited.

Are there many that wait?

There are more who have to wait than there are places available.

So is there a system of selection?

Yes, but it is still the individual who selects.

Which means?

You are presented with available options, and depending on where you are in your journey, you will choose the best course of action that will help to fulfil your potential.

It sounds a bit complicated.

It is a very difficult process to explain in words, or in any way that you might be able to fully comprehend, other than to say it is extremely organised. No one goes looking, and even if you are impatient you must still wait.

What about those who are impatient?

They simply accept what is available, even though it is unlikely there is little potential to be found by following the particular course and direction it may take them.

What about those who are all part of my family? How did we all choose this specific life and the direction it would take us?

You waited for a particular opportunity and were offered a part in the cycle that had been created around another group whose goal was greater than your own. There was potential in what they were attempting to achieve, which you thought might benefit you in your own particular areas of interest.

Had any of us shared in any other cycles before this?

In the immediate family yes, however you are all part of different strands and none of you form a prime element in your purpose for each of you being here. Two of you have shared more than the others, yet all this creates is a familiarity.

What about people in our lives with whom we are attached or may have a strong connection?

You will instinctively know if someone is strongly attached. In cases where there is a strong connection from a previous cycle it is often different, and there is a feeling that a part of you would be missing if something were to separate you. Of course you may feel this after long periods in a relationship, or a shared experience of an extremely emotional event, yet this does not necessarily constitute a connection from a previous cycle. Often this is a beginning in the formation of a new attachment, those with whom you may go on to create another union through further cycles of participation that will bind you even closer. For those with whom you have shared many cycles before, in a majority of cases they tend to be on the periphery of your main focus as opposed to any bonding involving family or birth. It simply depends on the direction and the purpose for which you are participating, and in this the reasons are numerous. You are all different, and there is no given rule that says you should do it like this or you must do it like that. All that is required is you experience a variety of different roles, and even this is by no means a rule, however it makes for a rounded pattern and potentially accelerates the overall process.

When you refer to a variety of different roles do you mean as either male or female?

It might appear to be an obvious conclusion, however there is more emphasis on relationships such as those that involve mother and father, parent and child, brother and sister.

And what about a relationship with someone we see more as an enemy than a friend?

If it is a relationship and there is a potential for advancement then nothing is excluded.

Are there any particular attachments we should try and avoid?

Every pattern that is part of the system has the potential to hold you at some point in your involvement, and some may last longer than others. It simply depends on the individual and the particular path they have chosen. The most common attachment involves a sexual element, however the most detrimental in terms of limiting an individual's progress is that which tends to illuminate a feeling of specialness, or the belief that you have somehow been set apart from everyone else. It has many strands and distortions that can show through in anything from the impression of beauty to the feeling of superiority. It is essentially a form of special love without substance, a feeling that you can acquire it without giving anything in return. Of all the parts that keep you focused on the illusion this is the greatest in terms of its potential to hold you in its light and prevent you from achieving your goal.

What are its consequences?

It is not that there is any specific consequence; just that it can have a negative effect on your progress, and often it may require the experience of various difficult cycles in order to emerge from the shadow of its perception.

We can't help it if some of us are more attractive or talented than others. Is that not simply part of the system of survival and how we form relationships?

It is one of the patterns that have grown from the system, but you will not grow by attaching yourself to them. You cannot take vanity with you, and even if you could it is not a pattern you would value.

Does that suggest we should avoid fame or any form of adulation?

It is not that you should avoid anything, and there are those who choose a particular cycle for this very purpose, not because they expect to lose themselves to the adulation of their talents or beauty, but in the challenge and their conviction that they will avoid it. For some it forms a specific element of their interest, and the fact that it provides greater temptation is the very reason they choose it.

And the temptations being what?

The illusion that it brings you something more than what it provides, or the possibility you may explore it at the expense of passing over the real purpose of your chosen course. In terms of all the choices and variations available it is not a direction one might pursue without being aware of the distractions or its potential to prolong your completion.

How would we best avoid this if we should find ourselves being tempted by the adulation of a special gift or talent?

By understanding it is only temporary and putting yourself in the position of those that direct the adulation. Know always that there is beauty in everything and a variety of talents in all that pursue a path of expression through the system of life that you are participating. Even if their beauty cannot be appreciated, or their talents may not be evident, you have nothing more that the other could not also have if this is what they had wished. Your brother had a talent for communication with those for whom the probabilities had been less fortunate, and even though this went largely unrecognised or unrewarded does not negate the fact that it existed. He was also a much greater musician than you have realised, and the very fact it also passed unknown does not in any way lessen his ability.

Could he have made something more of his music?

The truth is he was recognised for this ability in a previous cycle and paid a heavy price for the attachments it created, and the fact that nothing came of it in this one was more by his own design than the hand of fortune.

Spirituality and the Illusion

Is there anything we can do to accelerate our progress in life, or escape the illusion?

Know just that, it is an illusion.

But most people are convinced that this is all that exists.

And in their perception of certainty it is all that exists, they simply do not see the reality that underlies their continuation or makes it appear so absolute, but what you often fail to realise is that this is also the nature of the design.

Is that not a contradiction? In one hand we are told to be more spiritual and in connection with who we really are, and on the other hand you are saying it has been designed in such a way as to make us believe this is the only thing that exists.

The contradiction lies with the assumption that we have suggested you should become more spiritual, and in your reference to the term 'spiritual' we must also assume that you are referring to a certain level of understanding that will release you from the effects of the system. However there is very little you can do that will alter the pattern and release you from its experience, and to do so would negate its very purpose and the reasons you participate. You are here now in this time and place because this is what you have chosen, and from that choice you have also accepted the parameters that are responsible for the restrictions in your perception. It may be a difficult concept for you to accept but the truth is there is no level of awareness with respect to your reality that you can attain which will make it any different.

Then how can we accept it as an illusion, and even if we do, how will it help us to escape or accelerate our progress?

I am not suggesting it is easy, and the very fact that many cannot accept it is testament to the level of design. However the first thing required before any realisation can begin to surface is a desire to understand. Without this there is little anyone can do or say that will make you see it any differently. Even in those environments that many reside between the cycles of life cannot be convinced there is anything beyond the system in which they are participating.

How does the desire to understand help us to accept it as an illusion?

Because in your desire to understand you have created the first step of intention to see a way out, and the only way out of any system is through the same way you came in, and in this instance what brought you to this pattern of existence was a desire.

And the reason we cannot see it any differently is because we still maintain the desire to see it as it is?

Yet the reason you continue to see it as it is, including the potentials it provides is because you see value in the experience.

Is this what is meant when they say that there is always a part of the illusion we are unwilling to relinquish?

They are your attachments and what holds you in its light, and without the desire to relinquish them you will not see through the illusion to the part of reality from which it is being created.

So what you are basically saying then is there is very little we can do to accelerate our progress?

You will always be provided with the opportunities to know the truth, but there is nothing you will achieve without a genuine desire to achieve it.

But how can we possibly have a desire to achieve something if we don't know what that something is?

There is always another way, but you are unlikely to look for it while you are still mesmerised by the direction in which you are currently focused.

And what will happen when we are no longer captured by the pattern and the direction it is taking us?

Every so often you are given a reason to question the surroundings of your reality. It may only be fleeting in recognition, and last no longer than it takes to be distracted by another thought, but it is an opening in awareness, and a beginning in the process that will eventually lead you out of the dream, however you will not see it unless there is a genuine desire to do so.

Is there any sort of role, either individually or as a group we can play in the process?

You are always an option, or as we prefer, a variable that has the potential to encourage another to look in a different direction. As we have said one cannot help but be affected by those with whom we come into contact with, even if it may appear you have made little difference. However when it is time, or they are given a moment to question then there is always potential. It may only be a seed in the process of many more cycles, but it is a beginning and one that will grow in intensity. When they are ready then in your own awakening you will always be a light that will show them the way.

So we must essentially play out the course until such a moment arrives when it no longer interests us?

Why would you want to leave something that interests you, that you have chosen for your own intents and purposes?

I suppose because for all the potentials it provides it can also bring with it a lot of pain and misery.

And it is with some of this pain and misery that you are often concentrated that also has the potential to bring you some of its greatest joy.

Regardless of our love for life and all that it provides I think there are very few of us who finds any joy in misery.

That depends on which side of the experience you are looking at. If it is your own then you are simply focused on a particular strand or outcome, and while you are unwilling to avert your attention away from the experience that holds you in this state, then you are unlikely to see anything more. The most common cause of ones internal suffering is often the perception of change, or an event you cannot affect. Yet the potential for change is one of the primary reasons we choose to participate in a system with such a diverse selection of choice and direction. Our only fear, if it can be described as such is the state of unchanging, and all we covet is movement, because without movement we cannot finish what we have set out to achieve. With those who are very much lost to the system the difficulty with change is that in the intrinsic need to survive, they fear it will take them in a direction that will affect their ability to do so. In this need to survive I am not only referring to its basic elements, but in every aspect of life in which it surfaces. If it is not your work or your home, then it is your family, your relationships and your possessions. In your youth you are so immersed with the desire to participate in the system that you want nothing more than the opportunity to change, to create and build your own defences, and with age you begin to fear it because you are afraid that change will somehow take them away. However no matter how high you build your paper walls in the hope they will defend you from the effects of the system, it will always change, and this is what gives cause to your misery and why it grows with each passing year. Yet this is its joy, and although it may seem to promise you something you fear, it is the cycle of change that has the potential to provide you with everything you have wished.

What if that misery has been created by a state of unchanging? When nothing seems to be happening and all you want is movement?

In the act of creation there is always movement, and even when it appears otherwise it is simply because you are concentrated on an element that has not changed as much as you would have liked, but turn away and you will see that nearly everything around it has. You think little has changed in the last two years yet look within yourself and tell me what part of you is the same as it was then? Whether you like it or not, your misery is self-created and self perceived, and not because things haven't changed but because of the very fact that they have. You may not see it and perhaps you will disagree but there is nothing of your past that you would want, except perhaps for that which you believed was helping you to survive. However the fact remains you have managed perfectly well with the changes that have taken place and you will continue to do so for a long while to come.

What about someone else's misery?

If you are compelled to empathise with another's misery then know you have come a long way in your journey towards fulfilling your potential. The question is, can you help to alleviate that person's misery or make a difference? Unfortunately the answer is you cannot. It may not prevent you from trying, and perhaps you will even think that your efforts have made a difference, however this is often a distortion of your own desire, or the result of their own intention.

So what you are essentially saying is that there is nothing we can do to help alleviate someone else's suffering?

You may try, and there are many who derive a great deal of fulfilment from their efforts, but you must accept that, regardless of the circumstances, you all create your own reality. Whether that reality shows itself as either joy or misery, it is still a matter of perception, as it is your perception that they are suffering.

Yet in a majority of cases it is quite clear that people are suffering.

And what is clear for us here is that they have also created it, and if it shows itself through a particular course or event in which it appears they have no control, then know this is simply one of the challenges they have also chosen.

What about things like war, starvation, or the recession we are all witnessing?

No one is a victim of circumstance. If there is a course that plays itself out into a particular event it is the result of various probabilities, and from these probabilities there is always an opportunity to choose. For all those who were compelled to cancel the flights leading up to the events in September 2001 there were as many who were compelled to take them. Although the system does not often allow for the alteration of a particular action or event, there is always the option in which you may choose to participate or refrain. You only perceive these events in the shadow of a catastrophe you would like to have avoided, just as you would like to have avoided the atrocities and suffering of two great wars, but that is the nature of the system. There are probabilities in which neither of these events occurred, yet as it is they happened in this one, and you have grown much from having witnessed the effects, but for all those whose lives have been affected by these events there was a choice.

Even though they cannot consciously remember making that choice?

Just like you cannot consciously remember any of the choices that brought you here now, but like we say you are more than what you realise. In your original question you asked if there was anything more you can do to accelerate your progress and the answer is very little, and the reason for this is because there was very little required of you in the first place. You may suffer and witness the suffering of others in various degrees of intensity, yet all that matters is your reaction, because in the action born of reaction there is always change, and where there is change there is always the potential for joy.

Then what you are saying is that misery can bring joy?

Your misery is your reaction, however it is in the changes this reaction creates that will bring you joy.

But no one chooses to die?

Consciously no, even for us the very thought is a preposterous idea, but that is because in reality you cannot die, and because your unconscious reality is well aware that your departure from this world does not actually result in any death it is able to make the choice.

So because the idea of dying isn't something we can accept, it has to be chosen by the subconscious?

It is the entity as a whole that chooses, and another part that brings it into being. The most difficult aspect we are trying to convey is that you cannot accept there is a greater part of yourself with whom you are attached, even though you could not exist without it.

And it is this greater part that makes the choice?

Yes, but it is simply part of the design that in time you will grow to understand. The fact remains you are all as spiritual as you ever can be, and all that exists between the various elements of your identity from which a choice is made is the level of your awareness. The illusion is simply an experience you are responding to, and if you could perceive as another perceives it you will understand why it is that many react in the way they do. However if you can forgive them without giving mind to what you have forgiven, then you are at a level of awareness you are unlikely to surpass while you are a participant of the design.

The Attraction to Events (9/11)

It is difficult to accept everything that happens to us, good or bad, is something we have chosen.

That is because it is difficult to accept you are the cause of your own creations. If this was not true then maybe you would be at the effect of something in which you had no control, but the fact remains you are not. You control the course and direction of your own life in every way, and if you do not choose it then know you have created it.

How does that work then with an incident like the atrocities of 9/11? What was created and what was chosen?

The event is the consequence of a combined creative effort by its perpetrators, and the choice is taken by those who wish to be a part of the experience.

It is difficult to conceive that so many people in one location would choose to be a part of such a catastrophic event.

If you were given the option to die from a seemingly random everyday occurrence or from one that would change the course of history then, which would you choose?

From everything I have come to understand about the events surrounding that particular day I think I would have chosen the random everyday occurrence.

Even if that random everyday occurrence would be slow and lingering, so that those whose memories of you would diminish along with your physical and mental health? If one were to be given a conscious choice there are many who might not think this to be such an attractive proposition.

What if there was something you felt needed to be addressed, or if there was something you wanted to say before your departure? Given the choice most people would want time to reflect.

That is only because you think you will not be given a moment to do so beforehand.

And are we?

If there is something you wished to convey before you were finished that might help another in their own course and direction then you will be provided with the opportunity.

Even though you are not consciously aware of the fact that you are going to die?

There are many stories about people who unconsciously react to unseen events such as the mother who is compelled to entrust a cherished heirloom to her child or the brother who spontaneously returns the letters you once wrote him when you were young.

Are these unconscious reactions to the fact that their life would soon be finished?

They have completed their course and so there is little potential to be gained by continuing. In many instances but unknown to many of their friends and family they are often in pain, and there is no desire to prolong it any more than is necessary.

If someone's life was to suddenly end without warning perhaps they have missed an opportunity to put things right.

It is often those you leave behind that are given reason to regret, because it is only they who will remain closed to the realities of what lies beyond your existence. Yet perhaps in this scenario there is something about themselves they will not have previously recognised, something that will also help them in their own growth and completion. In many instances there is the potential to grow more from death than there is from life itself, and not just for those to whom it befalls but for everyone it has the potential to affect. Whether your departure is in disaster or in peace there is always a part of the course you have set out in which something can be learned from death.

How did those who died in the disaster of 9/11 choose to be a part of it?

The most important thing you must understand about the relationship between choice and its attachment to a particular event is that the human mind is unable to comprehend time as anything but a sequential phenomenon. The reality you cannot understand is that time is a layered simultaneous procedure that is connected through various points of similarity. In other words they are not connected by any sequence of time, even if this is how it might appear, but by a relationship of attraction.

I don't fully understand but I get the part about attraction.

Then we shall progress further until you understand why it is connected with creation. Every event that has been experienced has been created from a single thought. Somewhere in some place and from someone's mind it began its cycle as a simple idea. Now this idea is just the beginning of various possibilities in which it might grow and play out in a number of directions, however, the longer it is held the greater its ability to attract other minds to its potential. Yet even this does not ensure it will play out as it was originally conceived, indeed it may play out totally different from its original intention or it may not play out at all, but for the moment we will assume the beginnings of an event. Now this event is subject to the same probabilities as everything else, just as we were subject to the probabilities of our own creation. If you can imagine then for a moment you have booked to go on a journey in three years time, the fact that there is so much activity to contend with between now and the intention to travel it is by no means certain you will travel at all. However, the closer your journey becomes a reality the less chance there is that probability will play its part to prevent it. If you were to book your journey tomorrow then there is every reason to expect you will take it. This was the same for the events surrounding September 2001, and although you are not aware, it was one of many similar ideas that were given life by the same perpetrators, however by the same law of probability they did not play out as they were originally conceived. From all the ideas involving an attack this was the only one that came to fruition, yet even this did not play out as it was originally intended. Now as this idea gathered momentum towards becoming a reality it began to attract those who would share in an element of its creation. They will not have been consciously aware of it, but somewhere closer towards the actual event it had already been decided that their cycle was to end.

So the decision then becomes aligned with a particular event in which the outcome is shared?

And in this instance that particular outcome happened to be those of September 2001.

But what if that particular event was to result in the destruction of an entire country, or an attack that came from something like a genetically modified disease that could wipe out the population of the planet.

It would not have been allowed to travel any further than the idea, as it would affect the overall plan.

But this event was.

Yes, but it was the lesser of various different plans that originated from the same group.

So does that suggest you can interfere with the creation of an event?

We can interfere only in certain areas and if it compromises the choices of someone with whom we have a vested interest.

And what sort of things can you do?

We can protect them from the effects of the event.

What about the event itself?

We have no control. It is only with those who oversee the system that maintain the ability to alter the course and probability of a particular course and direction.

And when do they do this?

When there is a possibility that it will affect the overall system, or it is contrary to theirs and everybody else's interests.

So then at some level our choices can be compromised?

Only if it is contrary to the choices of everyone it has the potential to affect. You may do what you will in the course and direction of your own life, and if that choice happens to be a conscious decision to take your own life then there are those who will even help you to achieve it, but you cannot impose your will upon another who does not accept it. It is a basic law of the system and the environments that surround it. Choose what you will for yourself but you cannot choose for another.

Yet it could be argued that people impose their will on others all the time?

And it can also be argued that you only perceive it that way.

And what of those who do try to impose their will onto others, including the perpetrators of 9/11?

They must learn to accept the errors in their belief that they could do so.

And how will they do this?

They are aware of the errors surrounding their part, and for some of those involved it may require the experience of many cycles, but it will depend on the individual and the circumstances surrounding their actions.

Will those cycles be difficult?

They will be as difficult and challenging as they wish to make them. No one knows how you will choose to overcome the perception of certain failings in a cycle that results in the suffering of others, and until you can understand the circumstances of each individual you cannot guess at the choices they will make. However it would be wise to remember that many of these perpetrators were also the victims of another's attempt to impose their will.

What of atonement?

If you are asking if they will make amends for their actions then the answer is no, but this does not suggest there are no regrets, or a realisation that perhaps they had veered too greatly from their course, as there are for those who deliberately and needlessly kill another or take their own life.

So there is no atonement for your sins after life?

There is no form of judgement except for that with which you judge yourself. We are not suggesting a difficult journey does not await the perpetrators of suffering, and there is every reason to expect this might be the case, however it will be of their own choosing and for a reason they have accepted. If that happens to be a life in which they will encounter a similar experience to one they have imposed on another then it will come from their own intents and purposes, and not as a result of any previous action or reaction. You are always free to choose, but the choice is only affective within the parameters of the system in which you are participating.

You mean we cannot go back in time or choose to grow a finger if perhaps we were to lose one in an accident?

But you could have chosen not to participate in a particular action in which the finger was lost, just as you may choose to participate in a particular event in which you will die. The reason you do not comprehend the option of choice is because you fail to recognise that you are more than what you have consciously accepted.

And is there a way in which we could consciously accept it?

Look at your skin as it heals itself from a wound, or the movement of your body as it instantaneously and simultaneously responds to your thoughts, or better still take notice of the images you dream of at night. They are all clues to the expansive nature of your being, and even if you choose not to notice it does not lessen its purpose to help you in the direction and expression of life.

Prisoners of Consequence

Do our thoughts create who we are?

Your thoughts are merely the passing images of perception, and although they provide an insight into the process of your emotional reactions, alone they do not reflect who you are.

But if we are not our thoughts then how do we create our own reality?

I am not suggesting that your thoughts do not play some part in the eventual creation of your experience, but in and of themselves they are ineffectual. If the opposite were true then you would not make it past your front door each morning. Your thoughts are simply part of a process, however it is the manner in which they ignite a desire in you that creates your reality.

So it is our desire and not our thoughts that form the basis for our experience?

As I have previously stated, you experience nothing that you have not wished.

So for instance a man who is serving a prison sentence for robbery has he at some point wished for this?

He has wished for what he thought the robbery might bring him.

But he didn't wish for the consequences.

Yet he knew what they were! Now I am not saying that your desire creates a specific outcome, and the reason you are here in this particular cycle and that of your imaginary prisoner is testament to the fact that it doesn't, but the process by which it came alive began its journey with a desire. However this does not suggest the specific outcome that gave birth to your idea will not come to fruition at some point in your journey, just that it hasn't come to fruition yet, nor will it necessarily be as you had expected.

And what about the prisoner?

He acted upon a desire to attain a specific goal for which he went to prison, yet his desire for that specific goal is still very much alive, and when he is free he will probably maintain every intention to pursue it, perhaps in a different way, or maybe the same way that took him to prison. The fact remains he has created and continues to create his own reality.

And what about the possible environment he grew up in, does this not play a part in how or why he reacted to his desire. Perhaps he simply wanted something different, something better and maybe he just didn't know any other way to go about achieving it.

Yet he chose that environment.

But why would he choose such a life that lacked the opportunity to change it?

For the same reason we choose most things, for the challenge and the potentials it provides. Whichever way you perceive the reaction to life, everything in reality is given birth through desire. It may not always be easy to understand, and for those with whom it appears to create a lot of misery it is even more so. As is often the case in these situations, the outcome of their desire becomes distorted to such an extent that it goes beyond their ability to actually recognise it, but somewhere beneath the layers and patterns of their behaviour there exists a seed of desire for something they believed a particular action would bring them. For many they cannot even remember what it is they hoped their action would bring, but somewhere there is a preferred outcome, and in that outcome there is an intense desire to attain it.

Is that the same for everything we experience?

In a manner of speaking yes, but in the light of any particular experience it invariably comes from a desire for something else. The key to maintaining the integrity of your desire is not to be distracted by the way it might show itself and hold firm to the way you think it should.

Now I'm confused.

In your pursuit of a goal you have an image of what you think that goal might bring you, but what you do not know, at least in the beginning of the process is how you will go about attaining it. This is the same for all of us, including all of those who are participating in this system, but as is often the case we get better with each attempt. The difficulty is that from each experience you also create the potential to become distracted. It is this distraction that veers us from an original chosen course and direction, because from the distraction we begin to create a desire for something else, which in turn creates another distraction and another desire and so forth, until eventually you forget what it is that precipitated your action in the first place. If we look at our imaginary prisoner we can see that he has created his own reality from a particular desire, but for the most part he disagrees, and for the most part we can understand why, because who would wish for such a scenario that would have taken him to prison? However somewhere in the sequence of events that took him there we will find a desire, not for prison obviously, or even the action that precipitated the outcome, but somewhere at some point in which his desire and intention to attain it was ignited. It may have been a particular lifestyle, a certain person or perhaps some element of what that person was doing that he valued. Whatever the reason we must assume it began with a desire for something else other than the one it became, and we must also assume that its original purpose was for something much more positive.

How does a situation that takes you to prison begin with something more positive?

Because in the original action they believed it would

create a choice that was not available to them before they took it.

So you mean his desire or wish was to create more choices?

In a restricted environment is it not the impetus for most action and reaction?

Yet he has ended up in a situation in which he has even fewer choices than he had before.

Which gives us greater cause to sympathise with his predicament. It is similar to a budgie that might continuously trap itself in the feeder attached to a cage in which it cannot move.

I suppose he is trying to escape?

He wants more choices than those that are available to him in the cage, and so he keeps taking a course of action in which it appears he ends up with less. Of course this is not his intention, and it might amuse the observer because of the amount of times he will repeat the same action, however in the environment of his cage, it is the only course of action available to him. He has a desire for greater choice but somehow ends up with less, yet the fact is eventually he will get what he wants.

I don't understand.

There is a similar story you are aware of in which the owner, tired of his seeming stupidity, returned the budgie to his original owner, and once again he shared an aviary with dozens of other similar birds. Now in this case his desire for change and greater freedom of choice than the aviary originally provided took him on a course in which it seemed he was going backwards. In the care of his new owner he was restricted even more and in a smaller cage, but the fact is it eventually provided the impetus with which he would eventually escape. In this case the difficulty with his original desire to escape the aviary was his fear of human presence, but in a smaller cage and in which he had to be handled each time he got stuck in the food hatch he eventually overcame it. On being returned to the aviary of his beginnings he became bold and stayed near the opening whenever the owner came in to feed them or do otherwise, until eventually he took his opportunity and flew away. Now in the case of our imaginary prisoner, and like many others who might find themselves in a similar situation, he was already restricted in the environment from which he began the sequence of actions that eventually took him to prison.

And although it might appear that he has created less than he hoped, it will eventually bring him the outcome he originally desired?

In an ideal scenario this is what we would like to happen, however as you are well aware this is not always the case. For many the reality is that it will likely require the participation of many more cycles and repetitive actions before they will arrive at the outcome of their chosen destination.

Is this the same reason for say someone who is addicted to drugs, and while under the influence he gets into a fight that takes him to prison?

In this instance we may be inclined to explore another scenario. Let us assume that his drug addiction has evolved from his attempt to try and expand his options and create choice through the experience of drugs, because in his perception of others who take them it appears to offer a sense of freedom he cannot find in life. However the fact is that far from being free they are actually prisoners of their own addiction and he comes to realise it.   Therefore his experience of prison is a manifestation of that realisation.

But it doesn't deter him from taking drugs.

That is because he finds solace amongst those who feel the same way. If anything his experience of prison may simply reinforce his mistrust in what you would consider being the normalities of life to create an even greater dependency than before.

I'm finding it hard to see where his desire fits in with this?

That's because it was a manifestation of his reality.

So therefore if I'm in a situation in which I feel trapped, or I'm utterly frustrated...!

Then you will find yourself in a situation, or a series of events that will manifest those feelings.

But that is not a desire.

No, it is an actuality and you have simply created an environment around how you feel.

Yet if we are talking about how we create our own reality then what you are saying is that there is a difference between one that is borne out of desire and the other which has emerged to reflect how we feel?

Yes, in that one is a direction and the other is a projection. In the story of our imaginary prisoner his situation is the result of his direction, whereas with the drug addict it is a projection. In the case of the addict his internment is not the result of any premeditated action, yet with our imaginary prisoner it was the result of a robbery that had emerged from a desired outcome.

So when we create our own reality it is a two-strand affair?

No, it is a one-strand affair involving the direction of your desire and intention, whereas the other is simply a manifestation of what is.

What is the difference?

One is the consequence of your desire and intention to act, while the other is a projection of your emotional state. The major difference between them is that the projection of your emotions will change with your emotion, while the consequences of your action will not. Now I am not suggesting that the projection of your emotions does not cause you to act or react in a certain way, and if you do then you will still have to deal with the consequences of that action, but there is a difference. The key to understanding the circumstances of your situation is noticing it. Alone your thoughts do not create your experience nor do they define who you are. Just as your children may think of becoming a pirate or dying in the throes of a momentous battle with their arch enemy, you may think of robbing a bank or having an illustrious affair with a neighbour or a famous actress. You might even contemplate a hundred different unlawful ways in which you would deal with someone you dislike, however these do not suggest you are either a thief, an adulterer or a murderer, just as you do not think of your children as either a pirate or a war monger.

And yet we are supposed to beat ourselves up for thinking them?

That is because you have not yet come to appreciate they are simply a way in which you try to make sense of your environment. How could you make a choice without the ability to use your thoughts and explore an alternative? You are by nature an imaginative being, and we are all the products of an imaginative creator, but we are not our imaginings, even if it appears for a moment that we are. We may explore them and create from them an assortment of patterns in which we will lose ourselves, but we will not be lost in them forever, and for the short moments when it appears that we are, it will be of our own choosing and borne from a desire to explore them. Think what you will and explore them in your mind, and in the greatest detail if you feel the need, but know that unless you act upon them they are nothing more than a passing reflection of your will to create.

What of fantasy and thoughts we would rather not have?

Rejoice that you are in a position to fantasise and know that if you would rather not have them then you wouldn't.

Does that not simply encourage us to act them out?

On the contrary it should encourage you not to act them out, because if there is one thing we are certain, there is nothing you can actually create in your reality that cannot be experienced in your imagination. The greatest disappointment often awaits those who try to recreate and replicate the fields of their imagining, and not simply because they are beyond the limitations of the system in which they are attempting to create them.

But you could argue that most of us are simply trying to recreate our imaginings.

Only when you think that in your attempts to replicate them there is value in what they will achieve, but there is always a consequence.

So what should we keep as fantasy and what should we try and recreate?

Create that which will benefit and fantasise about that which will not.

So it would be okay to fantasise about having an adulterous affair so long as we don't act upon it?

What would be the consequence if you didn't?

I just think it is asking for trouble because, as is often the case, if you think about anything long enough you will just want to try and bring it to life.

And did the boy become a pirate, or come to death as he tried to slay his arch enemy? It is only in your attempt to suppress your fantasies that you are in danger of acting upon them, and by trying to convince someone it is wrong will only fuel the fire of their imaginings. It is quite true there are more who struggle with sin than those who do not believe in any.

Is that because they try to suppress it?

Yes, and by the nature of your attempts to do so you are keeping them to the forefront of your mind.

But the difference is that the child pirate gets to act out his fantasy of walking the plank and slaying his enemy.

That is because he is allowed to do so without consequence or ridicule. You accept that he is simply playing out a role in his imagination and it is encouraged, yet even if it wasn't he would still play them out in his mind and with the same sense of satisfaction as if it were real. It is the same for adults, however because you are of an age when those imaginings might be sexual in nature it is discouraged, yet it is for this reason it is more important than at any other time in your life.

Why is it so important?

Because of the sexual element that is an inherent part of the species and its perpetual need for an outlet. Whether you like it or not there is no individual who is sexually actualised that does not fantasise in the areas in which they are orientated.

Is this normal?

It is unlikely you could go on to achieve anything else if it were not.

Then why is it discouraged, and why are we made to feel bad for thinking certain things regarding our sexuality and orientation.

Because society has come to believe that everything wrong with the world is the result of it, when in fact it is simply the basis of the system that makes it what it is. You cannot repress the nature of the species. You may direct it and make of it what you will through both your imaginings and your reaction, but you cannot hide from the fact that it is a primary element of what you are. The key to dealing with what you might describe as the urges of sexual orientation is not to make of it anything more than what it is. To do so will simply create an attachment to the system that has no conclusion beyond that for which it was designed.

Yet so much is made of it, and almost everything we look at in life has been designed in such a way as to make us think it is everything.

When it is nothing more than an element of the urge to survive.

Isn't that a major element in the design of life on earth?

Yes part of it, but there are other elements of the design that are more important. The point is you are not your thoughts, and no matter how creatively you explore the fantasies of your imagination it does not impact in any way on the course and direction of your life, unless of course you choose to act upon them. In relation to the direction you follow it is of your own choosing, as are the consequences, and whether you perceive them as positive or not. If you are not content with a particular element of your life then it is within your power to change it, and the only reason it might sometimes appear difficult to do so is because you are to contend with the consequences of a previous choice.

Sexuality and Orientation

Do we choose our sexual orientation?

In the majority of cases yes, although it is possible that a particular orientation from a previous cycle can bleed through and will either confuse or distort the direction upon which it is aimed. It is rare but it happens.

So if you were previously a female and then choose to be a male then it has the potential to show through?

In a manner of speaking yes!

Is that the cause of homosexuality and the specifics of gender preference?

In some instances it is a bleed through from another cycle, while for others it can be an overdeveloped element of the personality borne out of many experiences in the same role as either male or female. However in the majority of cases it is a choice made by the individual prior to participation.

Is there any particular reason we might choose to do this?

Sometimes it is designed to aid the individual in the

pursuit of a particular goal. Another reason but less common is the challenge of overcoming an element that is not so easily accepted by other forms of society. However generally it is often a choice for those who embark on a course in which they wish to explore various facets of the human experience. As it is with most choices the reasons are numerous and individual to those who choose them.

Is it not difficult to assimilate yourself with each new cycle of life if you are used to being one way or another?

I can understand why it is you would think so, but it is not as difficult as you might expect, and the reason for this is because it is very much determined by the adopted form. Before this and afterwards there is no orientation one way or the other, unless of course there is an element of it with which you are particularly attached. The male and female aspect of the human species is specific only to the design, and with each integration you will adopt the pattern of preference for which it is directed. In most cases the integration is seamless and without notice, yet there are some for whom it is a little more difficult. In reality you are neither male nor female, yet in the pattern of life you have the propensity to express elements of both. Whichever way it is perceived the pattern of male and female is simply one of the many restrictions inherent in the design, yet unlike the other restrictions it is in fact one from which you can easily escape, if you so desired of course. The purpose of its design is the perception of two halves in order to instigate the action of union between them, and as you are no doubt aware, it forms a primary element of the game. Some might think it is the only element of the game, but that is simply because they are lost in its preoccupation. Obviously it also forms a major factor in the continuation of the species, but generally the male and female divide is only one of many different ways in which the primary purpose can be attained. Therefore sexuality and orientation makes little difference in the scheme of things, because whatever your leanings it is only the impetus in which you look for completion. Not forgetting of course that while you are a part of the illusion it cannot actually be attained.

So what you are saying is that apart from procreation it makes little difference which way we are sexually orientated?

It can make a difference to those for whom it affects, particularly in certain societies and if it goes against the mainstream of acceptance, but in terms of your growth and direction it has little affect. In some instances it may even accelerate your progress, but generally it makes little difference. Now in terms of orientation I am not only referring to what is considered normal in reference to procreation or homosexuality, I am speaking of any direction in which one might lean. As I have proclaimed you are not your thoughts, and you are also not a product of your sexuality either. It is simply a driving force that is inherent in the form you have adopted and one of the many restrictions and limitations you have to contend with.

What do you mean when you say it is an element of the design we could easily escape?

If you take into account all the elements of the illusion you are obliged to accept as reality, it is one in which you do not have to indulge.

I don't understand.

You must eat and stay warm, you must shelter and breathe, you must protect and be protected, and of course you must live or you will die. In all of these things you are obliged to participate, and not to do so would probably precipitate the end of your cycle, but in the drive to procreate and form a union it makes little difference if you choose to participate or not.

Yes but it is a drive we find difficult to control, and it wouldn't be easy.

It would prove far easier than if you chose not to eat or protect yourself. Now I am not suggesting it is something anyone would willingly choose to abstain from, even though there are many that do, just that if you chose to do so then the option is available. Fortunately it is not so readily available if for instance you chose not to breathe, although it will be so in due course, only the option beyond this is certain to take you in one direction.

There are some people among us who might not find that so amusing.

Amusing it might be, and deliberately intended also, but the fact that it will happen cannot be argued. Yet from my perception the humour is slightly elevated because it is imbued with the knowledge that it does not result in the end of your awareness, while for many it is only the beginning.

What did you mean when you said that while we are part of the illusion we will not find completion?

The part of you that is missing and which drives you to

look for it in your relationships cannot be reunited in the realms of the illusion. It will not lessen your willingness to try. As you are in no doubt aware the search for compatibility is a primary element of the game, yet it can also be argued it is a primary element of the illusion. Now I am not suggesting that you would fare better if you attempted to complete the cycle alone, because it is quite clear there is much to be gained if you did not, however in the forming of a relationship, be it of a sexual nature or otherwise it can never be the union you had wished.

Is this why monks and nuns choose to abstain from mainstream life and relationships?

They may think this is what they are doing when in fact they are simply continuing the system of survival and all it implies, but in the confines of a smaller group who share a similar intent. In actuality their bonding to one another is often much greater than it is in the world outside from which they are attempting to abstain. The fact remains you cannot escape the system by turning away from it, even if it appears that you can, and if anything the very act of trying enhances the potential to hold you in its light even longer than if you had bathed in it. The reason for this is because you are creating an extremity in the game that is sometimes greater than the extremity of the system itself. For those who choose this course it is often because there is a desire to experience the limitations it imposes on them and some may grow much for having done so, but generally they are creating an even greater challenge than this particular lifestyle attempts to avoid.

But they are in essence escaping an element of the illusion?

Yes but often they are also attempting to escape everything else, either consciously or otherwise. If you choose to relinquish the hold of your sexual orientation you do not have to become a monk or a nun to do so.

Are they not also attempting to remove the element of temptation and attraction?

Do you think a monk does not fantasise or a nun is without the ability to be attracted?

Yes but they put themselves in a position where it is often removed from their daily experience?

You cannot remove yourself from the part of you that yearns for union and compatibility. Like I have said, the very act of trying will only ignite in you the flame of intention, which is to grow and emerge from the system through the bonding of minds. There are some that may appear to succeed, but they are not any closer to their goal, and in many instances they may find themselves further from it than they had hoped.

Then what you are saying is we can abstain from the reaction to our sexual preferences but it is not going to benefit us, not in the long term at least?

What I am saying is the bonding of minds and that which you derive from a shared relationship does not require any element of sexual attraction. Some of the greatest expressions of love between two people are often created without any form of intimacy.

So what about our attraction to others?

There would be few of the potentials the system provides without it, however attraction is the impetus to create and not make love, even though you have come to believe differently. There are many whom you are attracted to, male and female, but it does not suggest any sexual connotation. In some instances it may be generated from the association, but for many it is not. You have simply evolved to focus on that from which a sexual connection has or can be created. The point is you are quite able to love and be loved without the need for intimacy. Now I am not attempting to reduce the importance of intimacy, as it can be a wonderful feeling for those who experience it, but it does not necessarily play any part in the forming of a relationship.

Surely attraction creates the desire to be intimate?

Most adults are attracted to children, both your own and that of others and for no other reason than the inherent desire to protect them. Now with this form of attraction you are inclined to hold them and kiss their rosy cheeks, and for those less intimate there is a desire to stroke their hair or touch their faces and it is an accepted way in which you express a desire to nurture and care for the young. Now there are many instances when you may also feel the same way about adults both male and female, and not just for those with whom you are familiar. They may be an acquaintance, a friend or a relative, and there are times you wish to stroke their cheeks or touch their hair, and not because of any sexual chemistry or with the hope it may lead to it, but because it is in the nature of who you are. However the fact is you do not and for reasons you are well aware, but it does not lessen the desire to do so.

The reason we don't do this is because of where it might lead or the potential that someone would take it the wrong way.

That is because you have grown accustomed to believing it is something more than what it is. There are many of you in long relationships that prefer such intimacy without the requirement of any sexual interaction, and I am not simply referring to the female element of the species, although it is true they do not possess the same drive as that which is imprisoned within the male. Of course it exists, just not with the same intensity or regularity of their opposite number.

So is it possible to enjoy a sexless marriage?

There are many that do but they would be loath to admit it for fear of being ridiculed by a society that has made a great deal more of it than it actually is. The fact remains you are perfectly capable of controlling the urges of sexual interaction, and there are many that do so. It is those who are lost to the body that it often proves to be a little more difficult, and not because they are less able to do so, but because they are merely victims of their own perception. By this I mean they only perceive the joys of their local environment. Whatever your sexual orientation, be it acceptable in society or not, in your imaginings there is nothing to be ashamed of, remembering of course it is only in your intention to act upon them that there is a consequence. Also keeping in mind the basic law of creation that you cannot impose your will upon another, either openly or through manipulation. Alone it has no bearing on the direction of association or kinships, and if you think that it does then you should look again at the purpose of your relationship.

The Opportunity to Act

Now with regards to creating your own reality there is something that requires a little clarification and must not be understated. When there is a desire and an intention of a particular intensity it will always generate various opportunities for the individual to act upon them.

So if the desire is strong enough it may tempt us into doing something about it, even if we might regret it?

It depends on the basis of your desire and intention. If it is to seduce a friend or steal from another then it could be portrayed as a temptation, however if it is to change your life or bring to fruition a particular dream or ambition then it is an opportunity. This does not diminish the effect of consequence if you choose to act, just that if the desire is strong enough then you will be provided with the circumstances in which to do so. I cannot emphasise enough the importance of this statement. Provided there is a desire to act then you will always be provided with the opportunity to act upon it. There are many circumstances of your life when it may appear this is not the case, or that perhaps there is little opportunity to escape the mundane existence of your surroundings, be it your work, family or the perceived restrictions imposed by obligation. However, the reason for this is you are simply focused on the situation of your experience, and unless you can construct a genuine alternative to ignite in you a desire or passion for something else then you will create few chances to affect your circumstance.

So if we are concentrated on the fact that perhaps we hate our job, the person we are living with or some area of our life then it will not change.

There is every possibility it will change just not in the way you had wished. It is simply the basics of choice in that if you do not choose then you can be certain that something or someone will come along and choose for you. The point I am making is that there is nothing in your life you cannot change, provided you have a desire and the passion to do so.

Then we are essentially a product of our desires.

Yet if the desire is not of a particular intensity then there is every possibility you will be the product of someone else's.

How does that relate to something like suffering or loneliness?

You are simply concentrated on the circumstances of your suffering or loneliness to the point of not giving the energy of mind towards a desired alternative.

What if we cannot see an alternative?

Then you will find little opportunity to change it, at least not in a way that you would prefer. Without the passion to seek out an alternative you would not even recognise the fact an opportunity had been presented.

Is this why we often find it more difficult to change things as we get older?

It is not any more difficult to create change in old age than it is in youth, but there is a greater reluctance to do so and therefore you are less flexible with the options available. In other words there is a desire for change but it is conditional.

There is always a part of the illusion we are unwilling to relinquish?

In these situations there is often no desire for anything else, and even when there is, you must still inject the energy of your imagination to provide an alternative. When you compare the passion of youth with that of age you will see where the difference arises.

Maybe as we get older there is little alternative that excites us enough to do anything about it?

It may be perceived this way, however we know this not to be the case. For many it is not so much about being excited enough to do anything about it, but because they either don't want to or they believe that they can't.

Why is it we nearly always seem to end up like this as we get older?

Because you become fearful that anything else may somehow be worse than what you have already accepted, that it might be less than you had hoped. Accept your misery in its current form and you will not change it, think positively and intently of something else and you will be given every opportunity to do so. It is simply the basics of choice in which you give energy to your creations, an idea made manifest from the desire to give it life. If you have ever aspired to understand the cause of suffering then know it only holds firm in your belief that there is nothing you can do to change it. It is with your dreams you must hold firm your passion for life, and even when sometimes your choices conspire to make less of them than you had hoped, it is only in your reluctance to finish the course that the dream begins to fade. I am not saying the sequence of experience that takes you on the path to its completion will not change what you had imagined, just that without your willingness to finish what you have begun you will never know what it might have been. Your passion for life does not simply die with age, it dies because you have no passion to change it, and the reason for this is because through time and your exposure to the system you are fearful of what it will bring. You had nothing more in youth than what you have now, even though it may seem that you did. The fact remains you would have died many more times as a boy than you would have done so in age, but what helped you to maintain your interest in life was an intensive desire to change it, and you did, and you have been doing so ever since. What may surprise you is that you have changed more in mind and with your feelings for life in the last twelve months than at any time in the last twenty years, and the reason for this is because something came along and forced an alteration.

But that wasn't out of choice but necessity. I had no control of what was happening.

Yet before this you were already dead, and in this I mean you were dead to any form of stimulus or passion that yearned for something different. The fact remains that only through necessity will many of you change your situation. As you have begun to realise, it was not so much the misfortune you had guessed, but a blessing and one in which you are now beginning to thrive.

But we all want to change things, even though circumstances may conspire to force that change, we just don't know how to do it or what we want instead.

And so you do nothing, therefore the force of creation, including the potentials it can provide conspires to do nothing about it also. There is much that can be done to assist you in achieving a particular goal, we can even place you in a direction that will take you straight to your destination, but what we cannot do is be your imagination, or ignite in you the desire or passion that will bring it to life. You have at your disposal everything that is required to make a reality come true, but you cannot make it without a dream, and just as you had once dreamed of everything you have now, the process does not end in its attainment. Like the long distance runner at the end of a race, provided she maintains a desire to compete, there will always be a race for her to run. In other words, just because you may be content in the completion of a goal does not mean you will always be content with what you have achieved, because that is the nature of creation and why the patterns of illusion will never end. As you are aware they did not begin with this experience in which you are currently focused and they will not end in its completion.   The reality of all consciousness and its perpetual desire to grow is that the beginning is always in the end. In your attempts to change your situation you have been active in the pursuit of various different goals but you have been disappointed that very little has come from your efforts, and the reason for this is because there was no real interest in making anything of them to begin with. It is quite obvious you have enjoyed the activity, however your expectation was not aligned with any real intention or desire, but with that of need.

But if you are hungry and you need food then it is only natural you are going to desire a situation in which it will be provided.

Yes but there is a difference in that the desire is borne out of a situation. The energy of desire required to positively affect your reality must come with the joy and imagination of what that reality should be. The reason you will not find fulfilment in a situation of need is because it may take you anywhere in which that need will be satisfied, and the very act of needing is simply giving life to the illusion that something is being deprived.

You mean that one is generated by a positive intention to create or change something while the other has come from a negative reaction to circumstance?

And from that reaction you erroneously create a goal you have no real desire of pursuing. If there hadn't been any negative effect in your circumstances it is unlikely you would have considered the many goals you hoped would help to change it let alone pursue them as a genuine alternative. As it is you did and nothing came from them, or was anything ever likely to, and not through any lack of willingness, intention or creativity, but because you had no real idea of what it is you hoped they would bring.

I hoped they would bring about change.

And yet they never did, at least not in a way that had any noticeable effect. However you may find it ironic that when you turned your attention to the area of your career which had been most affected by the situation the change you had wished for was almost immediate.

Why was this?

Because you had a clear picture of what you hoped your efforts would bring. Prior to this it had rarely crossed your mind because originally the changes in your circumstances hadn't actually affected anything. However once they began to affect your life you began to realise you had lost something, and because you had maintained a clear understanding of what it was you had lost, you had little difficulty in conjuring up an image of what it was you wished to bring back.

So therefore it is in my ability to conjure up an image of what it was that I wanted that made the difference?

Desire and intention will create the opportunity to change, but without the imagination of what it is you would have instead there is no definition of what that change might be. If you want choice then you must at least know what it is you would choose.

But there are lots of people that simply don't know. They are unhappy but they genuinely don't know what to do about it.

Then they cannot expect their situation to change, and unless they can look up from their experience and see a genuine alternative then it is unlikely they ever will.

So how do you help someone in this type of situation?

By being an alternative, an option or variation to what they are experiencing. You cannot make anyone look up from their situation or predicament, let alone help them change it, but you will always be an alternative when they are ready to do so. Do not focus on what it is you do not have, but imagine what it is you would have instead, and provided you inject into your imaginings the intensity of desire then know you will always be given the opportunity in which to bring them to life.

Unknown Civilisations

With reference to the pattern of human existence as we currently understand it, was it created by design or has it evolved to be this way?

That depends on your interpretation of the word evolve. If it is by means of adding significance to any sort of Darwinian theory of evolution then you misunderstand the complexities of your creation. If however it is by way of implying the introduction of additional patterns to that from which it was originally designed then yes it has evolved.

In what way has it evolved?

There are a number of experiences to which you apply a particular value, such as illusionary goals that light up an illusionary worth, or the feeling of specialness that can be attained with a specific talent or ability that another has been denied. These are all additions to the original pattern that have grown in significance, however they have little value beyond the system in which you pursue them.

We are all imbued with various talents and abilities.

Yes but not for the purpose of gaining anything more, or

to be set apart with a special goal, but to assist in the creation of a shared endeavour to survive the system. It is with the belief they can bring you more than this that a number of these patterns have been added. We are specifically interested in this aspect of the design and it forms a primary element in our decision to participate.

But you said these new patterns have only created an illusionary worth.

They have created an illusionary worth within the system, but this does suggest they are worthless. They form the basis of our interest but they have no value beyond the pattern in which they were created. They are simply additional layers you have added to the model that have conspired to forge an illusionary worth and reinforce your attachment.

Was there ever a time in human history when we existed without these additional patterns in which we seem to be so attached.

A very long time ago at the inception of your creation, and many thousands of years before any records of your current history, or the history before that.

How long ago was the human pattern first introduced here on earth?

Around one hundred thousand years ago, although the experiment of the human experience was introduced some three million years before, but not for any length of time or in large enough numbers to create any sort of elaborate community. It was essentially a practice period in preparation for their inception. During this time they coexisted with three other intelligent species until they were fully integrated into the system.

How would you describe these early stages of our existence?

Very much as the hunter-gatherer you know about but in small groups. As you might suspect much of their existence was focused on the system of survival as it was designed, however they were not completely lost to it as you are now in that they maintained a close affiliation and understanding of their origins. In other words they respected the system as it had been designed and were very much aware of an existence in the hierarchy of their creation.

You mean in the chain of survival?

Not so much in the hierarchy of survival but in their respect and acceptance that something existed beyond it. There was life before life and there would be life after it, and not just by way of a belief but also with a genuine understanding and conviction that there was. Now it may appear this would make little difference, but in terms of acceptance and how they lived life it made for a completely different reaction to their experience than what exists now.

Is that because they knew it wasn't real?

The concept of reality and illusion is that whatever your impression of life and the nature of your being there is no permanent effect. In other words you will always exist as part of the plan that is the fountain of creation and growth regardless of any outcome. So therefore it was very real, just as it is real for you now, but it was in their understanding that there was something beyond it that made the difference.   Now despite the lack of any technological awareness that would help to shield them from the effects of the system they accepted the impermanence of form and participated willingly in the pattern of existence without the fears you are now aware.   Therefore their reaction to death was not as emotional as it would later become.   This is not to say they were not emotionally affected by the experience, just not with the same intensity of loss as it is now. Overall it made for an enlightening experience, certainly more so than what you are currently accustomed to. They still maintained the elements of aggression required to exist and hold their own in the chain of survival, just not with the same intensity or destructiveness of the civilisations that would later follow. In other words they had not added the patterns of achievement and materialism to it that would eventually grow and become a primary element of their existence.

But they still participated in the system of survival?

They could not have existed otherwise, however they were respectful of it and accepted their part in the process.

What about the other intelligent species with whom they coexisted?

There were those you refer to as the Neanderthal and another race not dissimilar in appearance to yourselves and whose remains you have often mistaken for an evolutionary element of the human species.   However there was also a race of beings that existed here long before even these that we refer to as the Sleepers, but they were different.

In what way were they different?

In both their appearance and awareness, and they were not bound by the same restrictions as the others with whom they were required to share the environment.

Does that mean they had greater freedom?

They maintained a particular level of awareness and so were not required to participate in the system of survival, at least not in the way you might understand.

Why will I not understand?

Because their pattern of endeavour was not aligned with anything you would recognise. They shared the environment but were not of it in that they could come and go as they pleased.

But this was still their home?

Yes, but it wasn't their only home, just as it isn't yours, the difference being they were aware of it and you are not.

And what of this other species? Were there any other similarities that went beyond their appearance?

They were far more aggressive and less compromising in their outlook, and although their existence had been shared with the Sleepers it was more of an overlap in participation and there was little interaction between them. In many respects they were a prelude to the human intervention but they were different.

If they were more aggressive then how did the humans prevail?

They were singular in their objectives and their communities were small, whereas the humans were more sociable and eventually began to congregate in larger numbers, and it was with these qualities they came to dominate the system.

And what happened to this more aggressive type? Did they simply die out?

Yes, except for a small number that had been slowly integrated into the human pattern, however it was the end of their cycle, as it was for the Sleepers, while the Neanderthals were simply victims of a changing pattern of hierarchy. They were part of an earlier experiment but they found it difficult to grow or add anything of significance to the system.

Did the human inception have anything to do with the demise of the Sleepers?

It was simply their time. They had completed their course and there was little more they could have achieved by staying. They only remained out of curiosity and to assist with the integration of the new race.

How did they assist them?

They shared with them various elements of technology that were instrumental in the development of earlier human civilisations of which you are not aware, but it was misused and culminated in their demise many centuries after the Sleepers had left.

What sort of technology did they share?

They introduced them to instruments that could manipulate physical matter using the frequency of sound, which the Sleepers had used to create their underground cities. They also shared with them various secrets of electricity and electro magnetism, but again it was either misused or misunderstood and simply instigated a system of dominance and division.

Why have we never found any of these underground cities or examples of this technology?

Clues exist all over the world in the shape and movement of rocks and other large structures, however with the exception of the more durable elements many have been eroded to be almost indistinguishable from the surroundings in which they were created. Some of the finest examples now lie beneath the ocean surface or are rendered invisible by the shifting sands. It is the same for many of the human civilisations you are not aware of, both similar and more advanced in terms of their technological achievements, and despite your certainty there is every possibility you may even follow the same path of anonymity. Like everything that has gone before and those that are destined to take their place they will simply flow and recede with the cycles in which they were designed. Even though you cannot see them or hear their song does not mean they are dead to all sound and perception, because they have all contributed to the system an element of their existence. You may not have any knowledge of the Sleepers and you may question the significance of your Neanderthal and their persecutors but they have each added their part to the design and what it will eventually become. There may appear to be no connection between you in either body or mind, and on the surface of your genetic embellishment there isn't any, but this does not detract from what they have given or the direction of those that followed them. It is natural you may only see value in your own individual achievements but they are your ancestors in more ways than you can imagine, because even the slightest addition to the plan forms an integral part of what you are and what you will become. They may no longer exist to all forms of physical sense and perception but they paved the way for your integration, and whether you agree or not they are still very much part of the pattern.

In terms of these other species are we genetically similar?

Yes, but only because that is the system of coding upon which you were all created, however generally you are all different. Yet despite those differences you have all shared and continue to share in the goal for which the system was designed, and in this you are all eternally bonded.

What happened to all the other lost human civilisations we are not aware of?

Like those you know of from your recent past, they petered out, were consumed by another civilisation or receded with the changing cycles of the planet.

Is that just a polite way of saying they were wiped out by a natural catastrophe?

In some instances this was the case, but most were merely dissolved through the acts of migration and climatic extremes, as it will also conspire to dissolve the civilisations and cultures of today and in futures to come.

But what happened to this technology?

It was used in the creation of other civilisations and for thousands of years, and it had even evolved to inspire the development of other technological advances, but in the dissolution of each society that had benefited from its use it slowly became the preserve of a select number of chosen individuals. It would be much the same for your own civilisation if such erosion were to occur. Your technicians, scientists and doctors would quickly rise in status in line with the additional demand for their services, and as the situation would deteriorate into a system in which your value determined your chances of survival, it would create a greater reluctance to share the knowledge of their particular skills. It was the same for these civilisations that were lost, yet as with most things that are left in the hands of only a few chosen individuals, there is always a greater possibility that what they know will also be lost. In some cases it was the knowledge possessed by another society that many wars were often fought, and yet all this did was reinforce the will of those who possessed it to make it even more selective, because if nothing more it would guarantee their survival, or the potential to rise another day. Yet despite the dissolution of these ancient civilisations and the many conflicts that ensued to preserve ones advantage, much of this technology, or the knowledge of it at least existed up until six thousand years ago.

In the scheme of our currently known history that wasn't very long ago.

There are many structures visible around the world today that your scientists and archaeologists have allocated to a particular period and civilisation, when in fact they belong to another and from a much earlier existence. It is the same for some of the pyramids in Egypt and other structures you have found it difficult to allocate because they do not conform to your perception of their technological limitations. They were in fact created by a society that existed up until around five thousand years before the Egyptians arrived. In a majority of cases the Egyptians simply made alterations and tried to repair them as they deteriorated, yet the major elements surrounding the structure and design was the work of another civilisation.

Were they created for any specific purpose?

Yes, they provided a functional element to the landscape and were designed to deflect and redirect certain radio waves and frequencies. Particular shapes, sizes and locations provided a different function using the technology of sound. However, because a major element of their capacity lay in the material in which the structures were coated it is difficult for you to understand how they functioned, or appreciate their effect on the surroundings in which they were placed.

Can you explain some of this technology?

Sound waves were used to manipulate the molecular structure of physical matter. At its best it assisted in the creation of large elaborate structures and was able to eradicate the effects of cancerous cells, while at its worst it could be utilised to destroy entire cities and their populations. There were very few who fully appreciated its capability, and often in their attempts at destruction they invariably destroyed themselves. In later societies their lack of understanding in how the technology actually worked slowly began to reduce its potential and the ways in which it could effectively be used.

And how did the Egyptians use this technology?

It was utilised in numerous forms of society from the elimination of various illnesses and disease to the practice of initiating certain states of consciousness. Its knowledge was a primary reason for the rising status of the priesthood in their society that had empowered them to overrule or instigate certain laws and decrees that were often unpopular.

Is there anything in their history we know about that might give us some clues as to its effects and how it was used?

There is barely enough to provide any overwhelming evidence that will convince your archaeologists and scientists, however it would help if you were to decipher in more detail the symbols of their art, particularly the earlier examples. You will find little knowledge or understanding of their society in the design and construction of the pyramids because they belong to a much earlier civilisation; although it is possible you may find clues in them to the importance of sound, which they had adopted as the basis for their society and ritualistic endeavours. You may also find clues in this technology through your earliest texts and the mysteries surrounding the Exodus of the Jews, including the Arc of the Covenant.

Was it with the use of this technology that caused the walls of Jericho to crumble?

It is one of many stories that makes reference to it, however by this time it had been altered, and although there were some human civilisations that possessed a complete knowledge and understanding of how it worked, in a majority of cases it was greatly diminished from its actual potential.

Yet despite that knowledge it still managed to disappear and be eradicated from history?

Despite everything you have a desire to create, it will always exist within a world of impermanence. You think that since little has changed in three thousand years it perhaps gives you a sense of stability and belief of how it is or how it will always be, yet in the life of the planet and the greater part of your experience it is the briefest of moments. Some of these lost civilisations existed for much longer than this, and yet not only have they dissolved without providing any clues of their actual existence, so have the numerous patterns they had inspired within various other societies around the planet. I am not suggesting that the basis of your current society and its achievements will not survive the various cycles of the planet, but unless you can adapt either your thinking or certain beliefs regarding the nature and purpose of your creation then it is highly unlikely.

Is this why there is nothing left of these other civilisations?

Their technology was misused, and they still believed in the body as the primary purpose of their endeavour, whereas its original creators did not. It was the same for the Egyptians who devised various rituals involving the preservation of their mummified bodies, however they still could not accept the possibility of an existence beyond that which they could only see with their eyes, while the Mayans sacrificed their young to appease an imaginary God. There were roads and cities from the past like you have now, and structures of science even more detailed and elaborate than you might imagine, but their creators still could not see beyond themselves, much the same way that most cannot see beyond what they are now. You have created the Theory of Relativity and split an atom but still many believe that everything in life and its myriad designs have all evolved from a random primordial soup, even though it would suggest to have done so would require the greatest odds of chance and fortune that the entire cosmos has ever known. Is it really possible this is the only known planet to miraculously turn at a particular axis and at a consistent point and distance from the sun for over three billion years without significant alteration? You have been balancing on a precipice since the earliest designs of life and still many do not know what it is that keeps you from falling into the abyss.

What about the patterns of life that existed before the humans, or the Sleepers before them?

It was very much as you have imagined, but it went through various stages of experimentation. The earliest designs in which attention was focused were those that grew from the earth, then the oceans, and then finally the complex life forms that were created to live in both.

And did any of these early life forms add any new patterns of their own?

Not in any way that was valued. There were some that were imbued with a similar capacity of intelligence as the human form, but their environment was restricted and they had little desire to venture any distance from the ocean.

They were ocean dwellers?

They were imbued with the ability to exist on both land and water, but it was with the ocean that they felt more secure. Although the system of survival was just as virulent as that being played out on land, they were far more adept at dealing with the one that existed in the ocean.

Were they as intelligent as we are now?

In some respects even more so, however their capacity was simply greater than their desire to venture any further from the original pattern they were given. They were not in any way simple and they had evolved to develop a complex structure within the water. There were very few predators of both the ocean and land that they were not capable of dealing with as a group, but without any desire to venture from the ocean there was little potential to grow or add to the system as it was hoped.

Were these ocean dwellers basically a stage in the experiment?

Essentially all early life forms were a stage in the experiment.

How many stages of experimentation did it go through?

In terms of major changes there were several stages, although numerous alterations were made in between.

Is that the reason behind the extinction of the dinosaurs and the various other major changes that effectively altered the history of life on earth?

They were periods of experimentation and observation in the pursuit of a particular goal. They were also elements of a changing environment and the attempts to maintain a particular balance in which all forms could coexist.

What was this particular goal they were pursuing?

The primary goal for the creation of life on earth is the generation and transformation of emotion.

And the system of survival provides every emotion imaginable?

On the contrary it may surprise you that it doesn't. For those involved it might seem that way, and in a majority of cases it will invoke a certain response, but this alone is not enough, nor is it an element of emotion that is particularly valued.

Is this why it went through so many stages of change and experimentation?

From the patterns that grew from the element of survival it was eventually transformed into the potentials of what it is now.

Which is the bonding of minds through the extremities of the system. All roads lead to Rome!

That is because in all roads and in all directions there is only one goal.

What I don't understand is that if there was no evolution as such, then in relation to these various stages of experimentation, did those who were responsible for its design simply come in at the end of each process and eliminate all life forms in order to make way for new ones?

I can understand why it might appear that way but this is not how it happened. The precipice over which you are finely balanced is only maintained because of external intervention, but at the end of these cycles it was simply left to play out its course.

Which resulted in the life forms from each stage of the process being wiped from the planet, hence the extinction of the dinosaurs and almost everything else with it.

Without intervention it is highly probable this is how it may end, but let us not forget there is also a probability that it will not, and it may surprise you to know that there are many examples of life from these initial stages of the experiment that still exist today. There is little joy in seeing the destruction of something you have created, even though the pattern of its existence is only an illusion, so it will always be provided with the opportunity to continue its presence in the environment for which it was designed. Yet not with any expectation it will die, but with every hope that it will live, because it is in the spontaneous reaction to change that can often provide us with the greatest potential to grow. Without the energy and commitment of its creators these designs of life could not have existed in the first place, but as it is they did, and so therefore they were given every opportunity to continue, just as the Sleepers, the Neanderthals and their persecutors were given the chance to coexist with the human inhabitants, even though there was little more they could achieve or add to the system. However unlike the new arrivals they did not have the protection of any external intervention. In other words they were left to play out their course.

What do you mean by the protection of external intervention?

The clusters of energy that would sponsor their existence and assist them in their endeavour no longer existed in any great numbers to make a difference.

They had left?

They were no longer focused on the patterns in which their interest had originally been ignited and there was little potential in taking it any further.

So their focus of attention, or interest had been diverted to the human pattern?

Yes, although participation in the human project essentially came from a different source and new clusters of energy.

And these clusters that are now involved with the human pattern, do they maintain the ability to intervene in the process if it is required?

It is not so much about our ability to intervene as opposed to the level of desire and intentions to do so, and very few maintained any desire to follow the course set out by either the Neanderthal or the Sleeper. The reason for this is because their pattern was complete and there was little more to be achieved with the addition of anything else.   A completed goal has little potential. There was always a chance that something may have evolved from interaction with the new species, and for quite a while there was, but not in any particular shape or with any intensity that made it worth pursuing further.

So with these other races that came before us there was no longer interest in their pattern of existence and now we continue where they left off?

Yes, but with different capabilities and in a new direction.

In what way are our capabilities different?

The Sleepers maintained a greater perception of their reality so they were less inclined to lose themselves to the system, and to a greater degree they managed to abstain from a large part of it, while the Neanderthal was essentially the opposite. In other words they had little or no comprehension of anything beyond their existence. The species of human comes somewhere in between, although closer to the Neanderthal than the Sleeper.

And what about the aggressors or persecutors that were similar to the humans?

In their original form they too died out, however through integration a variable form of human was created.

You mean different?

Not through any appearance or capability.   It merely shows itself in the structure of blood and through the elements you recognise as the negative. They are a form of hybrid of two similar species. They are different but not in any way that is noticeable except they have a propensity to be more aggressive and less compliant, yet not any more so than any human is capable of being either, just that there is a greater potential to manifest these particular traits.   Beyond this there is little difference, and you all follow the same course and direction.

There seems to be so much from the past that we know nothing about?

And there is so much of the future you have yet to witness. The fact remains you are not the first intelligent species to walk this planet, and there is nothing to say you are also alone in your endeavour, yet that is perhaps another story for another day, but what is certain is you will not be its last. As a species all that is important is you have added to the pattern and there is every reason to expect you will continue to do so for many years to come.

And when there is nothing more to add?

Then we will have finished our course and it will be time to move on.

Will that be the end of the human race as a species?

It is possible, yet it is also possible they will stay and create another sequence, or perhaps they will continue elsewhere with a new course and direction.

But it won't be with us, or our cluster to sponsor their existence?

Or with any of the other clusters who are currently attached to the human endeavour. I am not saying it is impossible, and for those who still wait on the completion of a sponsored form, it is unlikely they will leave without them.

Is there a timescale for our exodus?

Thirteen or fourteen hundred years, perhaps longer!

Yet in the scheme of everything we have been discussing it isn't very long.

Although it is much longer than the Mayans had prophesied.

Was that not simply the end of a calendar?

And the end of the world as they had believed, and yet in relation to the world in which they were referring, it ended much sooner than even they had imagined. Now I am not suggesting your own world will continue for the next fourteen hundred years in its current form, because there is every reason to expect that it will not, but it will continue.

Why is there every reason to expect it will not continue in its current form?

If the human endeavour were to continue in the same vain then you could be sure there would be little left for anything else.

So we should expect that something is going to change?

It is always changing, and while you maintain a sense of your own awareness it will continue to do so, but then is that not what we have just been discussing?

The Sequence of Time

You say it may take someone who is part of your cluster thousands of years and numerous cycles before they can relinquish their attachment to the pattern of life on earth. It seems like a long time for you to wait.

In our environment the perception of time is very different than what it is for you there. Unlike the direction that runs from the past into the future and which you are obliged to calculate the elements of change, our existence is measured between the various points of our growth. Therefore it is not so much about length but what we were, what we are and what we will become. For example in your mind it has been some time since we shared our thoughts, yet for me I have simply moved from our last exchange to this one, and from this one I will move to the next.

But for me so much has happened in between.

As it can also happen for us here, yet the difference between our two realities is that here we choose what it is that happens.

Do I not do the same?

Essentially yes, but if there is no exchange between us until next week then you cannot move from now straight to that point, whereas I can. For you and the illusion of time there is a sequence you must follow, and in terms of environmental restrictions it is one in which you are locked. Now there is also a sequence for us, however it does not follow any particular line or direction.

So when you say you may wait thousands of years for someone from your cluster to emerge from the experience of life, it doesn't actually mean you wait that long, at least not in the sense of time as it would appear to us?

No, because essentially there are no gaps in between each experience. You could also say there are no gaps in between your own experience, and the only reason it appears that way is because you are obliged to follow a particular sequence that you perceive as being linear. For us there is no such thing as a linear direction and there are more than three dimensions.

So if I were to live for say seventy years, for you it will appear much less?

Yes, and it is only a short time for you also, however it does not appear that way while you are lost in the illusion. For us Time is relative to our experience. You could say that in our desire to grow we are trying to create more time, and so therefore the greater we are in our experience the longer it would take for another to experience it.

As part of your cluster am I therefore adding to what you are?

Through your experiences in time, but in reality the distance between the events of your life, or the trivialities that appears to link them all together are non-existent, and in its completion you will be able to see them as a series of uninterrupted events, very much as we can see them now.

But if time does not exist for you there as it does for us here then how can you comprehend the events of our experience, which are essentially linear in their construction?

Exactly the same way as you do, yet we are not confined or held to follow any of the events in between, unless of course we choose to do so. You see the pattern of life has been designed so that its experience must follow a particular course, a little bit like a fairground ride that travels through an imaginary village or city. You must follow a particular path, or be carried along by the train, which has been designed to weave its way through the environment. You may be taken past an animated castle with various characters and characteristics, and then onto another part of the world that has been created for your enjoyment, but there is still a course and a direction that it must follow as it takes you from one place to the next. For us we experience the events much the same way but without the journey in between, and we can travel in whichever direction we choose. Now when this cycle is complete you too will also be able to view the entire experience in the same way, or you may view it in the sequence as it occurred.

So in a review of our life and without the trivialities in between it would appear like we have only lived for a short period?

When calculating the culmination of events you will value on the completion of your experience it is highly unlikely you will have lived any more than a day.

A day!   Is that all we will have to show for our endeavour?

In terms of the desire to grow and fulfil your potential it is all you will need.

But one day for an entire life?   It doesn't seem like very much.

You misunderstand; I am referring to a unit of one day to show the culmination of every lifetime and every experience you will have generated from your entire participation.

If you were to remove all the hours of our life we spend in sleep and going through the motions of thoughtless repetition then I can understand how it might be condensed, but that still leaves a whole chunk of our lives unaccounted for.

To begin with you are not dead to yourself while you sleep, and even though you may not remember the details it is still a valid element of the human experience, as is also the cycle of repetition, just that it is unlikely that you would want to repeat any of it.

Is that by way of implying it has no relevance?

It is all relevant, particularly if you wish to see how one event can lead to another, but in and of itself it does not have any value. If you wish to walk down a road for forty years and see the same things every day without any flicker of emotion or response then how much of that experience would you want to take with you?

But that wouldn't happen.

Yet many of you walk for long periods without any flicker of emotion or responding to the experience. Now I am not suggesting this has no relevance to the events which are scattered along the course of your life, because they are essentially the adhesive that binds them all together as one. However in relation to the elements of experience that gives it meaning it is merely part of the process and as such it has no intrinsic value.

So the movement of time, or the illusion of it, is simply a process by which we accumulate experience.

Or as you may prefer, it is a way of processing the information of your life. However the illusion of time still exists in the same manner in which the event is experienced, but for us here who are not bound by the process, the elements of experience are compressed. For example this communication, or exchange, is for you the culmination of various different events with lots of other experiences and events in between, for me it is simply one experience, and when your cycle is complete it will be the same for you also. In the process of living life and the way it has been constructed you may see a line leading from the past to the future with a beginning and an end that gives the impression of length. Now if you were to roll this line into a ball you will in fact see that there is no line at all, and if you were to compress that ball even further to remove everything that has no value, such as those periods you have walked without emotion or response, then in relation to the experience of life and the illusion of time in which it was constructed it makes for a very small ball.

So in the construction of our life, all those details, or those long periods we have walked without emotion are they lost?

It is not that anything in your life is lost, just the fabric of time in which it was experienced. Time is simply a framework that conspires to take you in a particular course and direction. Essentially it is the carousel of time that is the illusion, in which you enter and exit at various different points along its journey, and as it goes about its way the scenery is changing and you are changing with it.

You have previously said that when our cycle is over it is possible to review various probabilities of our life we could have chosen instead. How is that possible if you are no longer bound by the sequence of time in which it is experienced? I just don't understand how you can reduce the elements of someone's life into something so small.

Think of your life and everything that it comprises of being made into a film. Now in most cases a film does not exceed a running time of two hours, but in a majority of cases it is enough to reveal a story. Yet although it only runs for two hours, its creation has involved the combined effort of numerous individuals that would run into perhaps one hundred thousand hours. Now some of that time may have required hundreds of hours to film just one sequence, yet neither the audience, nor the director has any real desire to watch all of this, and for those who were involved in capturing this sequence it is highly unlikely they will want to repeat it either. However it was still a necessary requirement in producing the film. Now in response to your question, the movie, or the culminated events of your life is simply the condensed article, and in its completion it is this that the director will hold as verification to his accomplishments. Yet this does not negate the hundred thousand hours that were required to make the film, for the fact is that without this effort it could never have been made in the first place. However it was the end result that had inspired him to create the film and which he values.

So therefore it is only in the finished movie will the action of his endeavour be judged?

Not any form of judgement that involves a consequence, but one in which to validate his creation. Yet the hours involved with its production are not lost, and you do not have to live the entire story in minute detail, but if there is a desire to investigate specific elements of the film then you may do so.

Is this how it is for you there?

In a manner of speaking yes, and we do not have to unravel the reel of film to find what it is we are looking for. As for the specific details and individual associations involved in the creation of the movie, it is highly probable they are also part of another story, and the details of that story are a part of another as well, and so the tapestry continues, entwined in the tapestry of another and so forth. If your enthusiasm is of a particular intensity it is quite possible you may lose yourself for a very long period. Yet the possibility of losing yourself in this way is something that for the most part you are shielded, and the reason for this is because your limitations only allow you to travel in one direction. Now in terms of our communication, whenever I am obliged to delve into specific details it is possible I could be gone for a very long period, and in some instances I am, but you are not aware of it nor will you notice.

When I stop writing do you notice when I am gone?

Sometimes yes, but for the most part it is simply only a pause in our communication.

And what happens when you get distracted?

It may surprise you to know you are just such a distraction in that you began something that interested me, and it was from my desire to follow that interest that we are now having this conversation.

How did you become distracted?

Let us just say I was watching your movie when I became interested by a particular outcome, or the probability of it, but let us not get distracted by another strand of our topic, otherwise we might be here for a very long time.

So if all we will have for our entire participation in the pattern of life on earth through numerous cycles will not total any more than one day, then what does it require to make a cluster of energy?

A great deal more than the efforts to explore and grow

from a single strand of life.

Yet if all of my combined effort will only culminate in a day, then how old or how big is the cluster of which you and I are both a part?

A hundred years, perhaps more.

But that must be the culmination of thousands of lives?

As I have previously said, we are small in comparison. There are some who have the culmination of over a hundred thousand, and elsewhere there are clusters that are made up from the energy forms of an entire planet. Yet in many examples such as this a great deal of their make up will involve a certain amount of repetition, as it does for many of us who are focused on this particular pattern of endeavour, but with those who invest so much into one system it is even more so. I am not suggesting there is little value in a repetitious experience, because it is with repetition we become more skilled in defining our direction, however it is not something in which we are particularly interested.

Why is this?

It is from what we can add to the system that we will grow and achieve what is required before we can return. Now in terms of how little you grow from the participation of each cycle you may begin to understand why it is we are running out of time.

But if what you say is correct and we only have another thirteen or fourteen hundred years remaining then I cannot see how it will be enough.

If we were obliged to follow one direction then it is highly unlikely it will be, however we are fortunate that this is not the case.

I don't understand.

You are assuming that the process of participation goes in one direction from the past into the future.

You mean that someone's next cycle of life will not automatically occur sometime in the future?

Not necessarily.

But then that would contradict the process of growth in that, if we have come from there to here, how do we make good our intention, or follow a particular course if we were to go back again.

As a species in this timeline there is only one direction, and if as a species you have achieved your potential, it is no guarantee that you will have done so as an individual, and if that is the case then you may have no other choice but to consider another direction.

You mean that in terms of where I am now, possibly having to choose an existence sometime in the past?

Essentially yes.

But has the past not already happened? Have all the lives not already been lived and are someway responsible for who we are and where we are now?

A particular version of it exists yes, but there are still probabilities in which it may play out differently. A child who died at birth, or perhaps a life that was short lived. To alter an event in which another course of action would prevail has the potential to create an entire new strand of opportunities in which millions who had been lost to war or famine will have lived to provide an even greater host of opportunities for those who might also then live because of it.

You mean by way of creating more cycles of life that had otherwise been prevented because of a certain event?

Or perhaps less! The point I am making is that if it is required then the options are endless. Of course, in terms of a continuous timeline, it would be preferable if you were to follow the same course and direction, because essentially it is in the pursuit of a single path, or a line of history that we see our endeavours come to fruition. Perhaps not now, or in a hundred years, or maybe never, but there is always the potential that it might.

So taking a cycle of life in the past is not something we would do out of choice?

No, but it is possible, and there are some who will have good reason for doing so, while for those who run out of time it is likely they may have no other choice.

Is it possible for the clusters with whom we are all attached to instantaneously visit any point in our life? For example could you go straight to the point when I die?

Yes, however it would remove the potential to play a part in any of the events of your life that will occur between now and then. In other words I could not come back to this point now and continue with our communication. I could view the details of how it has played out without my input, and I could even view a probability of the event if I had stayed to complete our exchange, but I could not influence or have any affect on either outcome.

But if you were curious?

Curiosity would prevent me from experiencing the potentials in between, as it would you if you could fast forward to your point of exit now, not that you have any particular desire to do so. However if it was possible then it is also certain there would be little in between to miss out on.

So in some respects you are still bound by the illusion of time?

We are only bound by the restrictions of a system when we are focused on a particular life we have created that is a part of it, and if we wish to maintain the ability to affect or influence that life then to a lesser degree we must also accept those restrictions. You see the reason we follow you is because essentially we are one and the same, and we come alive to the system when you do, but we are not bound by the details in between. In other words we can do other things as well and in different directions.

But if you are to follow the life of someone you have created then you have to follow his or her sequence?

We don't have to follow anything, but we choose to, and if we wish to maintain the option to influence and experience the spontaneity of their reactions then we must follow the pattern as they are creating it.

What do you mean when you say you come alive to the system when I do?

When there is potential in your emotional responses then we are very much alive to them as you are.

Is this communication we are having now the result of an emotional response?

You know quite clearly that it is.

But there is no emotional reaction from me at this moment.

No, but there was and this is now the response, and the communication we are having is the consequence of our intervention.

Yet I am reminded of various emotional moments much earlier in my life when it was quite clear there was no intervention.

And we remember those events as if they took place yesterday.

That is because in light of what we have just been discussing, for you it probably was only yesterday.

In terms of how we experience the events of your life there is little distance between them, for us at least, therefore we probably have a greater understanding of them than you are capable of remembering. Yet, as we are both aware, these moments that you question our intervention were in fact the impetus for a more fulfilling experience and what eventually brought you to this point now.

What about something like a suicide attempt, do you respond?

If it is an attempt that fails then you may assume we have responded, yet even this may not be enough to prevent it from being repeated or its eventual outcome. However in some instances when a suicide attempt is destined to fail a response may not be required.

How would you know it was going to fail?

If we can see that there is an event beyond that of the attempted suicide then our intervention may not be required. In other words whatever the circumstances surrounding such an event it will be clear to us that nothing will come of it, in fact it may even be the impetus for a certain change that would have prevented the attempt.

Even if that change may not happen for another twenty years?

For us the unit of time has no affect on the value of change. Now I am not suggesting that the change will be positive, but if there is a probability then we will be aware of it. However if we wanted to advance to a point in that person's life and see it as it actually plays out then we will not be able to influence any of the events in between. We are of the moment but we see the points in which various probabilities of those moments might occur.

So you respond to all my emotional reactions?

It would make little sense to the purpose for which you were created if we didn't.   However it is not always in a way that you will notice, or in a timescale you might expect, but we always respond.

What if someone's emotional reaction has occurred because of a potential threat to his or her life?

If it is not what they have chosen, or a consequence of their actions then we will prevent it.

What if they are hit by a bus and there is no emotional reaction, or there is no time to respond?

There is always an emotional reaction, because what you do not realise is that they will have reacted beforehand to a probability that the bus was going to hit them.

And you respond to prevent it?

Or let it happen if it is a choice, or part of the plan, and the fact you have not yet been hit by a bus you may assume that we have responded.

So then what you are saying is that we can react emotionally to a probability?

You will react if there is a possibility that the event will take place. If a plane is soon to take off that will crash and you are booked to fly on it as a passenger then you will react to the probability you are going to be killed, and if it was not intended or something you have chosen then we will respond to prevent it. However if you are booked to sail on a boat in twelve months time that may sink, there is so much that can happen in between it is still highly likely that circumstances may conspire to prevent you from taking the journey. It simply depends on the probability that the event in question will actually take place.

And the timescale determines the possibility of it happening or not?

In most instances yes, but as is often the case it will simply depend on the details and the circumstances of each individual event.

The Cause of Ageing

What is the importance and value of emotion?

It is through emotion that you generate a specific level of energy that gives validity to the action of your existence. Without emotion, or the ability to generate it then you will not be exposed to the potentials for which the system was designed.

Even if that emotion is something like fear?

If you are fearful then you are validating the reality of your experience.

I don't understand.

The only way you could not be fearful is if you knew for certain that the experience was an illusion, but the fact that you are responding to it emotionally is testament to the fact that whatever you are reacting to must be real.

What would happen if we knew for certain that it wasn't real?

Then you would not react to it emotionally, and therefore you would also lack the potential to generate or transform the energy for which the pattern of life and its environment was designed.

Do we grow due to the generation of emotion?

In some respects yes, but it is not exclusively responsible. You will grow from the experience regardless, however it is through the generation of emotion and how you deal with it that your progress within the design is measured.

I don't quite understand?

The expression of life and the myriad patterns upon which it is made up is brought into existence by a specific band of energy. We on the other hand are made up from a different band of energy. If you were to go back far enough you would find that both energy strands have originated from a single source, however they have both developed to express different characteristics and varieties of potential. Presently this structure of energy that has been used for the creation of life on earth is something we are unfamiliar with. We understand the general elements, and we are not so unfamiliar that we are unable to assimilate ourselves with its design, hence the numerous clusters that do so, but it is not an energy form in which we are proficient. In other words we do not possess the skills or knowledge to create from it the expressions of life that you are currently aware, whereas those who designed it are.

You mean that the energy from which life is created is somewhat alien to us?

Not so much alien, because despite the contrasting potentials that exist between the two strands of energy they have both originated from the same source, however they have evolved differently, just as others have evolved differently to create a host of other patterns of which you are also not aware. However the energy that is responsible for the expression of physical life in the Universe, as you and I understand it, is specific to a particular strand. Now this band of energy has certain peculiarities in that it reacts to various stimuli, and in the creation of physical life one of those varieties of stimuli is emotion. Another peculiarity is that in its reaction to emotional stimuli it also transforms into something different, and depending on the level and intensity of the reaction there are a variety of ways in which it can be transformed. In terms of measuring your progress it is the manner in which you can transform this energy that is a primary factor in the design and one of the reasons you choose to participate.

What do you mean when you say there are a variety of patterns in which it can be transformed?

There are a variety of ways in which it can be transformed into another type of energy, and how it is transformed will determine how it reacts upon the system of life from which it was generated.

And how will it react?

That depends on the level and intensity of the emotion. At its worst it has the potential to affect and transform the cells of the life form in which it is generated, while at its best it can bring to life anything it comes into contact with.

If it can affect and transform the cells of the life form is that not another way of saying it can destroy you?

Essentially nothing can be destroyed, but in the process

by which it is transformed this is how it might appear.

So if we generate the wrong type of emotion then basically it has the potential to kill us?

If the emotion is of a particular intensity and generated for a specific period then yes, it can destroy the form that relies on its energy for expression. This is the primary reason why the physical body begins to age, because in the regeneration of your cells they are slowly being transformed by their exposure to the energy of emotion and therefore they become less stable.

Is this what causes cancer?

In relation to the cycles of life and its transformation it is the cause of most illnesses. Whether it is perceived as life or death, good or bad, right and wrong, it is the energy from which your environment comes into existence. Cancerous cells and the signals they create, although not specific to any type of negative emotion, are generally the effect of conflict.

For a system in which survival and conflict play a major part then does that mean by the very nature of our participation we are constantly exposed to the potential of destroying ourselves.

You are exposed to the illusion of destroying yourself! The challenge and the primary reason for which it was created is to generate a specific type of emotion in which it doesn't.

You mean love?

And any of its positive counterparts!

But in its natural form it is rare?

Like a scattering of white buttercups in a field of wheat. As I have said it is not easy but that is the challenge and one of the reasons we choose to participate.

So in terms of how little we value from the cycle of one life is it almost impossible to create any more?

The level and intensity of certain emotions you generate exposes the body to a form of energy it cannot withstand.

Hence the reason it takes so many cycles and why we have to keep coming back in a new body, because essentially it cannot cope.

It is in its current form that the body cannot cope, at least not for any length of time.

Could it cope better and for longer in a different form or expression of life?

Of course, and there was a period of human existence when you were quite capable and it was possible to live for much longer than what you consider to be a normal lifespan, but in a distant past that you are unaware of. You are simply concentrating your attention on the emotional energy from which the current human experience has a propensity to generate. With greater understanding of the system and a way of reacting to it differently it is possible to far exceed the number of years a human body can survive.

You mean by abstaining from negative emotion in which we find it difficult to withstand, but does that not contradict the purpose for which it was created?

You are simply focused on your perception of what it is and not the potentials of what it can be. Alone and misdirected the energy of emotion has the ability to negatively transform a whole planet, but with love and understanding it is possible to create an entire universe. It is with the potential to transform and create that is the primary reason for which this system and its patterns of life were designed, and not to destroy or dismantle the channels in which it flows.

In other words it is because of what we are doing with it now that it becomes destructive?

Essentially yes, and yet the only thing it is destroying is the pattern of life it is also responsible for creating.

So the purpose of life and the whole system that sustains it was designed to generate and transform the energy of emotion in order to recreate?

And also to share its potentials with other patterns so that they can grow.

And we are benefitting from that extension?

As we have been benefitting from various other patterns and their extensions since the beginning of our creation.

How does the band of energy used in the creation of life and the band of energy you and I are a part of differ?

The energy upon which you currently depend has the complexity and intensity to maintain the existence of physical life, whereas the band of energy of which we are a part is less complex. You could say that we are essentially part of the source in its original form, and the energy of life is a transformation of that source.

So the clusters of energy forms currently involved with life on earth have evolved differently from those who designed and created it?

The majority have evolved from a different spectrum of the energy field of which we are all a part, but here it is more concentrated, and it is this concentration that has the potential to create life.

Or destroy it?

It is those that adopt the energy who are responsible for their own destruction because they have yet to either understand or deal with it.

How would you deal with it?

By being careful how we would go about generating it, and abstaining from the masses in which it is concentrated even more.

Concentrated even more than it already is? Wouldn't that be suicidal?

If the concentrated energy is of a particular type and

intensity it has the potential to impact heavily on the body and quicken its degeneration.

Does that suggest if we were to congregate in a large crowd that was emotionally charged it would not be good for us?

Only if you were focused on the event that was the cause of the emotion and it was negatively charged.

So you would have to be focused on the event for it to have any effect?

If you were to walk through a rally, or a large gathering of people without any awareness as to the purpose of their interest it would have little impact.

So getting involved with a sporting event or a political rally that is emotionally charged isn't good for us?

Not unless you are detached from the outcome.

Is this the reason why political leaders and those in similar positions seem to age rapidly after they take office?

They are invariably involved with the concentrated emotions of an entire nation, however the most successful are those who maintain the ability to avert their focus.

Is it possible to do that?

Some are better at it than others, however it is those who are able to avert the focus of their awareness away from the negative elements of emotion that do not always recognise the potentials.

You mean they are cold?

It may appear that way, but often they are simply more skilled at re-aligning the receptive parts of their mind away from the energy of emotion.

Does that suggest that these types of people tend to make the best leaders?

And sometimes they tend to make your most prolific villains.

Is that because they are emotionally detached from the consequences of their actions?   That would explain a lot.

If you could understand it fully it would explain everything.

How do these particular people maintain the ability to avert their focus away from the emotional reactions of what is happening around them?

For some, it is something they have developed over many cycles, while for others it is a sense of perception, but for the most part it is an element in which they are naturally imbued at the inception of their creation.

Does this then imply that the clusters of energy that participate in this pattern of life are all different?

The majority of them are similar to us, but there are some who have evolved from the spectrum of energy upon which the system was created, and so therefore they are much more proficient in dealing with the variations.

If they are proficient then why do they participate?

For the same reason as we do, but they are different, and in many instances so are their interests. In terms of participation they are simply more proficient in dealing with the generation of emotional energy, which they have developed from their involvement in other similar patterns elsewhere. For the most part they are not particularly interested in this system because there is little potential, but there are some that are.

Are there any other types that are different?

There is one other, but we know little about them except to say they tend to concentrate their attention in a particular location, and they have little interest in the potentials for which it was created.

But are they still human?

Very much so, and they are still bound by the same laws and limitations that you all are, but their reasons for participating are different. Beyond this we do not know, except to say they are small in number.

So there are other energy fields?

There are numerous different spectrums of the energy field of which we are all a part, yet their focus and interests lie elsewhere, and there is little interaction or communication. There are many forms, many dimensions and an incalculable number of patterns that grow from them, and the energy upon which this particular system was created, including the patterns it reflects is simply one strand.

Is it possible you will ever be able to create a similar pattern, or a complex life system such as this?

It is something that we aspire to achieve but with another spectrum of energy.

I don't understand.   Why don't you just become proficient in this one?

Because many of its potentials have already been realised. It is how it can be added to and transformed into other patterns and in a new direction that forms a primary element of our intent.

And how will you do this?

Hopefully in the fusion of energies between that which creates this system and our own, but that is a long way from where we are at present, and there is no guarantee it will succeed.

What will happen if it doesn't succeed?

Then we will try again elsewhere in another system, or perhaps with a different spectrum of energy, but we are hopeful, and even if we have not succeeded when this particular pattern is complete, it is possible we may try again with it somewhere else.

Why not just continue with it here?

If we cannot achieve our goal in the time we have already

been allocated then there is little chance it will succeed if the opportunity were to be extended. Even if it was there are other factors to be considered, and there is a spectrum that waits for us to complete.

You mean a new race or a new pattern will replace the one that exists now?

We are unsure about the specific details, except to say it will follow a new direction.

Is the creation of another spectrum of energy the ultimate goal?

The ultimate goal is to grow and become more than we are. That is our only desire and intention, but it is through different potentials and the variations of creation can we achieve our goal.

And what happens beyond this, or when there is no more potential to grow or become more?

Until that moment arrives we are unsure except to say that another goal will arise beyond this, and beyond that also.

What if another goal does not arise?

Then we shall return from whence we came, through the aperture as one with all the other variations that have evolved from the original source, only transformed.

I think I finally understand. You evolve from one line with one purpose, and then you divide and then sub divide in all directions, and into many patterns. A bit like a line that divides into a fork and then returns in a sort of heart shaped fountain, returning to the flow, but transformed.   Yet the flow and the direction, where is it going?

Returning to the one that created it!

But for what reason did they create it?

For the same reason that we create everything, to grow and be transformed.

And beyond this perhaps another flow, and in another direction, constantly changing, and always from one place, the opening to which you refer to as the aperture.

We are pleased you are finally beginning to understand, however we have much to complete before we can contemplate this outcome, not least the one that brought us to this moment of communication.

In terms of life in the universe and what you are attempting to achieve it could take you billions of years.

Then it is just as well that we have all the time in the world, but in the meantime it would help if you did not get too emotional, at least not until you have learnt to deal with it.

That is very amusing.   In relation to the whole scheme of things it seems that I have drawn the short straw. On the one hand if I fully participate the emotion will kill me, and if I don't then I'll have to keep on coming back until it does. I'm going to need all the time in the world just to get through this.

You are doing better than you think, and you are simply focused on the negatives, because in the scattering of white buttercups you have had little exposure to its potentials, but from what you have created it will grow, as will your enthusiasm to accumulate even more.

The scattering of white buttercups! Why do you keep using this phrase?

You have yet to comprehend the symbolism of what we are attempting to portray?

Is it really so unique?

How many white buttercups have you seen?

That's my point, I haven't!

But you accept that a buttercup exists?

You are referring to their transformation! That is why you label them as being white, because they do not actually exist.

But in their current yellow form they are abundant.

I think I understand, and this is why they are so rare?

Would its creators have designed such a wonderfully

complex system of life and the myriad patterns in which it can be expressed if it wasn't so rare? In time you will grow to understand, as will your enthusiasm to complete what you have begun. For now you are perplexed by your perception of what it means, but through your endeavour it will change, and we will have grown from your interpretation.

But in the meantime it is here that I must concentrate my attention?

Until you have finished what you have begun there is nowhere else for you to go, at least not for now, but it waits, as do we in the knowledge it has all to be experienced.

How did we get from the energy of emotion to the purpose of creation?

As you have said, all roads lead to Rome. One purpose, one direction, and everything else is simply a division or a distortion of that plan.

Including the complexities involved in the energy of our creation?

Especially so, but that does not detract from the fact that this is where our attentions are currently directed, and until we are finished this is where they will remain.

Except to wonder where it is we are going.

And is that not the purpose of dreaming? Is that not also why we are here now unravelling what it is you wanted to know. Whatever we do and wherever we go it must always begin with a dream, even if we are not quite sure what the outcome of that dream will be it has to start somewhere, be it the aperture or somewhere else beyond. However for now you should concentrate your dreaming on the parts of your existence that you can see come alive and leave it for us to dream of where we shall go when they do.

In relation to the energy of emotion, if a certain transformation is responsible for ageing, then can another reverse the effects?

Yes, but it will take a great undertaking by the individual to reverse the manner in which the emotion that caused the damage is generated, as well as an understanding of his role in the way it is channelled. It may not necessary extend your cycle, but it would halt, reduce or reverse the effects of ageing.

Why do most animals age much faster then we do?

They are primarily involved in the negative form of emotion that represents the system of survival in which they are involved, and their cycle of procreation is also relative to a particular balance that must be maintained.

Is that also the same for us?

There would be nothing left of the system if it wasn't?

But we are different?

Provided you maintain the propensity for empathy and compassion then you will always be different.

Can animals have compassion?

Essentially no, and if sometimes it appears that they do then they are invariably responding to your own, because that is the power in which you are entrusted.

So is it possible for a compassionate man to live for longer?

He can be as compassionate as he is capable, but if he generates enough negative emotion it will make little difference. They are two different transformations and one does not cancel out the other.

Cycles of a Distant Planet

Are there any other worlds with a similar pattern of life to that which exists here on earth?

The variety of life forms with a similar capacity for intelligence and reasoning to that which you see in the human experience are numerous, as are the civilisations and patterns of existence that grow from them, yet we know of only two you may deem comparable to the system of life on earth.

In the whole universe there are only two that are similar?

We are referring to those with a similar environment and pattern of existence to that which exists here on earth.

And was there any likeness in appearance to us now?

With regards to shape and physiology yes, but in relation to size and facial appearances they were very different.

Have you participated in or experienced the cycles of life on any of these other worlds?

Our interest was essentially for observation, as it was for the system of life on earth before we became involved.

Was there any particular reason you did not become involved with these other two life forms?

Unfortunately one was coming towards the end of its existence, including the environment that sustained it, while the other had evolved to achieve such a high level of awareness and technology there was little potential to add or grow from any involvement. If we had been given the opportunity we would have chosen the world that was dying but it was too late.

What was it that interested you in this dying world or the species that inhabited it?

There was simplicity in the way they had evolved, and yet in terms of technology and their achievements it was extremely complex. However in relation to awareness they were not dissimilar to how you are now, but less aggressive and more versatile with their assimilation to the system of survival.

Which means?

They were less affected by the restrictions of their environment, or the element of survival that was similar to the one that exists here.

Were they more advanced than what we are now?

Yes but they had existed for much longer without the sequence of interruptions and changes that have become a familiar pattern of the human experience. There were changes and fluctuations involving various civilisations through which they had evolved, however their technological achievements were built on such clearly defined foundations that they were often carried through from one sequence to the next.

Yet in the evolution of the human race whatever advances we made were invariably lost.

However with this particular species it had grown and evolved through a sequence of change which had for a large part avoided any interruptions to the process.

So if the sequence in their technological progress was uninterrupted then for how long had it continuously evolved?

Towards the end of their existence it had continued uninterrupted for the equivalent of perhaps thirty thousands years. There were changes of course, and civilisations of various forms came and went very much as they have done here, yet little changed in the simplicity of their thinking from which a majority of their technological achievements had grown.

If they were so technologically advanced then why was it simple?

Their existence was essentially founded on a binary concept. They still maintained a capacity for more complex arrangements, however it was from the element of binary calculations upon which they preferred to create their complexity.

Did they have a vocal language similar to ours?

Yes, but it veered more towards the intonation of sound and pitch as opposed to the structure of words and sentencing as it has evolved with the human endeavour, however their variety of pitch and vibration was far greater than what you are capable of.

But they still used words?

To a degree yes, but not in a way that required them to create a dictionary. Their requirement for words was basically used by way of categorising their communication in which they would then elaborate using the sound and pitch of their voice, and although this was the primary form of communication it was also complimented by an intricate system of sign language. Yet despite this colourful aspect of communication the primary element of their thinking revolved around a method of choice in that nearly every aspect of their society, including direction, design and creativity had all evolved from a system of one and two. In other words it either went one way or the other, and almost every other pattern that might contrast with this binary way of thinking was rarely considered as an alternative. I am not saying it did not exist, just not in any way in which it would readily be applied, and was primarily reserved for artistic endeavours as opposed to any constructive design or engineering. Now with this binary way of thinking, far from encouraging any form of limitation with regards to capacity for growth actually gave rise to an extremely complex and sophisticated system of society as well as an intricate arrangement of technological achievements. The reason for this is because in the process of design and creation it greatly reduced the potential to become overwhelmed.

So how did this affect the way in which they had grown and evolved as opposed to our own?

The clarity in which everything was created made it much easier to add something more, or change it if it was required, and because the alterations were often small and without any noticeable effect they were allowed to grow.

Like the coral reefs beneath the surface of the ocean, they start with something small and modest, and then develop into a more complex pattern of life.

And also by adding small changes to any form of creation it has the potential to eliminate resistance.

But what if something in the system wasn't working, they would still have to contend with the same problems we are always being faced with?

If it wasn't working then it was relatively easy to retrace the design back to the juncture where it began to fail. The difficulty with the human system is that it has evolved from a mosaic like pattern in which a myriad options and directions are taken at once, and so whenever you are presented with situations or designs that aren't working it is often very difficult to make a change or alteration without impacting heavily on either the course or the creative element as a whole.

And so therefore we choose to do nothing as opposed to starting it all over again?

Or as history has often shown, you patch it up as best you can until it breaks down altogether.

Is that the reason why so many human civilisations have come and gone here on earth?

It is one of the reasons yes, and because an intricate pattern has emerged, when it is no longer working it is often too difficult to change or see where it has gone wrong.

Until eventually it collapses altogether, and this is probably what will happen to the civilisations that exist today.

That is the human system and one of the elements that attract those who become involved. It is a challenge, and even though it is difficult we choose it not so that we will fail but in the hope that eventually we will succeed. I am not suggesting this other race of beings were any less interesting, or that there were fewer potentials that exist here on earth, just that they were different, and in a way that attracted our interest.

Can you explain this difference in more detail?

A good example that conveys a pattern in their thinking was in the mode of travel and how they commuted between one place to the next. It consisted of a large intricate network of tubular structures above and below the surface of the planet in a variety of colours that were almost indestructible to every natural element except heat. However, unlike the various other modes of travel that now exist here on earth, it was the major transport network they all used and in which they could move rapidly from one side of the planet to the other in a relatively short time. In itself this network of tubes was not particularly unusual, yet on the surface it looked as complex and elaborate as anything you would create here on earth, but its mode of operation and the way it functioned was extremely simple and effective. For example there were very few intersections or junctions, yet whenever it was required it never exceeded the choice of two possible directions.

How did that work if you were at a centre point of say five or six different locations?

It would merely take one direction in which six separate locations could be exited one after the other.

They extended the network just so that they would avoid a junction or an intersection?

To have done it any other way would have created an assortment of other complications, not least to their own thought processes and the way the system was programmed to function, as well as the manner in which it serviced other elements of their society and existence.

So they weren't simply created for travel?

They were used for the transportation of everything required for their society to flourish, from food and goods to the distribution of light and energy. They still walked in the open air and utilised various other modes of transport including flight, but they were used primarily for the purpose of leisure and exploration as opposed to operating any major function with regards to society or travel.

How did the network function?

Inside the tubes were divided into two halves, each representing a direction, and depending on where someone or something was being directed, it would travel either along the upper half or lower half, with the outer sections used for the transportation of people and the inner portions being utilised for the distribution of almost everything else.

What if they wanted to move something really big?

The item would be designed in such a way that it could be distributed through the tubes and assembled at its destination. There were exceptions of course, particularly with elements involving hazardous materials, but generally everything was designed to travel through the tubular network, and to any destination on the planet without any changeover or interruption.

So it was a bit like the universally sized steel containers we use today for shipping goods all over the world?

Yes, but instead of waiting for the containers to be filled, each item, however small, could be sent immediately by anyone and reach its destination anywhere the same day, and wherever it was going to on the planet. In relation to your own transport network the whole system worked at an incredible speed and infiltrated almost every section of the planet where their civilisation flourished.

What if they wanted to send something or someone to a place where there was little interest or activity?

Apart from a few exceptions they would still travel through a network of tubes, even if they had to be temporarily constructed. Whichever direction, and for whatever purpose there was very little action that did not involve a tubular structure, hence the reason why we refer to them as the tubular race.

Still it must have been prone to the same potential to break down as our own networks, particularly if it was so intrinsically linked.

Sometimes there were complications, yet everything would merely be redirected on a route that would bypass the failure until it was rectified, but it was rare. They were very efficient at erecting new structures whenever an occasion required them to do so.

It must have been highly organised and extremely fast if it was used to service the needs of an entire planet?

It was as highly efficient and as fast as the minds that created it, and yet also straightforward in its mode of operation. Now the reason I am describing this network of transportation is because it typifies the way they thought and went about their daily lives. Whatever the skills, their structures and their creations they were all designed from a system of choosing one direction or another, however, like a great chess player with the capacity to plan several various different moves in advance, they could follow the potentials of numerous probabilities. Yet their success and technological achievements had been built on a system of finding the simplest solution.

What about maths and physics, or the complicated sciences in which we like to create elaborate theories that many of us rarely understand?

They existed just as they exist here, yet they were looked at and understood in a way that you are currently unable to comprehend. The human skill and capacity is in the way it can hold onto various strands of a pattern without being submerged or overwhelmed by the design. The tubular race did not possess such ability, and so therefore they could not have survived in a system such as this, however through a basic process of dissection they could elaborate on things that are often too difficult for you to understand. So with regards to maths, physics or science they were far more knowledgeable than you are, or likely to be for many centuries of progress to come, but that does not suggest it formed the basis for their technological achievements. Currently this might appear to be a contradiction, but as I have said their success was in seeking the option of simplicity. They were so creative with their ability to dissect and untangle the most complex designs they had conquered gravity and eliminated most diseases.

Surely there's nothing simple in that?

Simpler than you think, or as it was for them. Yet what they could not do was theorise, or create an idea from nothing.

But if it transpires that what you have theorised about is wrong, or not possible then some might say it wasn't worth creating a theory about it in the first place.

Yet you could also argue that the ability to theorise provides a number of advantages, and in some parts it is the potential to create from nothing that is most revered.

So this race of people, or this species did not have the capacity to create a theory about something they may not understand, like Darwin's Theory of Evolution, or Einstein's Theory of Relativity?

They probably understood the facts of both creation and light more than those you mention, but what they could not do was create a theory without a fact, in which case it is no longer a theory.

And how would they have responded to such theories?

They would analyse them and then furnish you with the facts.

Assuming they were able to do so.

If they couldn't then it is highly likely there was little fact or substance to be found in them.

Suddenly they are beginning to sound like a very interesting race of people.

We thought so too, and so far we have only spoken of an element of their technological achievements.

Did they express similar emotions to our own?

Yes, except anger, at least not in the negative manner in which you understand it. In other words, they felt anger but they could control it, and they did not react to it with aggression.

And if they had conquered gravity then they must have conquered space.

They had explored their solar system and a large section of what you would consider to be its local environment, but much of this was achieved from their attempt to find another planet to live. At the time of our observation their own world was rapidly fading in its ability to support life, and so therefore the requirement to find a possible replacement, temporary or permanent, was of primary importance.

Considering they were so advanced could they not have prepared better for the eventual death of their planet?

They were well aware of the impending situation thousands of years before any changes were expected to take affect. However the expansion of the sun and its erosion of the atmosphere was far more rapid than they had calculated, and by the time other alternatives had been found it was too late, for the majority at least.

When you say another alternative do you mean another planet?

Yes, but even these alternatives they had found were not really suitable, at least not for any prolonged period or for the numbers it would have to sustain.

So what happened to them?

By the time the explorers had returned with viable alternatives, apart from a small number who had managed to shield themselves from the worst affects, the entire population and its natural wildlife had perished from a systematic wave of cataclysmic disasters.

Why so quickly?

It was an inevitable outcome, yet the whole disintegration was much quicker than anyone could have estimated, and they had not expected the scale of natural catastrophe that the changing climate would cause. Those who had left in search of new worlds had been gone for hundreds of years, and when they had begun to return with viable alternatives they were not prepared for the scenario that greeted them. Yet even these new worlds they had marked out and returned to with the remaining population were not suitable, and eventually the entire species was destroyed by a natural cyclical catastrophe they also had little time to prepare for.

It all seems so sad, and yet I hardly know anything about them.

It is never easy to witness the demise of any race regardless of their achievements, and yet it is a natural process in the cycle of life and creation. It will most likely be the same for the human pattern of existence as it was for the various other species that existed before them, and for those that will come after, but not through the ending of a planet. To complete the pattern of expression with the environment that has supported it is extremely rare, and in most cases it is a privilege for the species that shares the experience.

And yet it is also emotionally sad.

Of course, but that is where much of the potential is derived.

The bonding of minds through a shared experience!

And what better way is there than sharing the completion of your cycle with the completion of an entire planet?

My empathy and curiosity would rather see it continue.

That is because you do not see the new worlds and the various new patterns that emerge from its completion. Where do you think you came from and the species before that, and before that also?

We started here.

It may surprise you to know it actually began somewhere else, and will most likely continue somewhere else when it is finished here, but in a different direction and with another purpose. As we have said nothing is lost, because there will always be a blueprint of creation and its environment however small and intricate, and if required it will be introduced, perhaps in another system with a different goal and intention, or maybe not, but it will always exist.

And the life of this tubular race is there a blueprint of everything that existed on their planet, and can it still be experienced?

Yes, but you could not add to the pattern they have completed, or change what it is or what it has been, nor would you want to.

Could they be brought back into existence somewhere else?

If there is potential then there is always a possibility.

But it no longer exists as an evolving system like ours?

What it can be it has been, and what it can give it has given, yet there was little else it could have been or they could have given that would have added anything more. There is much we could tell you with regard to their history, lifestyle and achievements, but there is little you will learn that cannot be learnt from your own participation and endeavour here. We only refer to them and a specific element with regards to their creative thought processes by way of providing you with a contrast to your own pattern of being, because somewhere in the story of their existence there is a lesson.

Which is?

No matter how you think of your experience, whether it is in relation to what you can see and feel, or perhaps the direction your life may be going, there is always another way, and despite any seeming complexity, it is often so clear as not to appear obvious. Now you are eager to ask us about the other race we have observed, but by way of providing you with another contrast to your own way of being their story is much more complicated, and there is little desire on your behalf to tackle the intricacies. There is an enthusiasm to know, but you do not currently possess the quietness of mind to know it, so we will share it with you by way of an appendix at a later date, and yet if the truth were to be known, it is a story with which you are already familiar.

Now I am intrigued.

Then let us hope you will maintain that intrigue until you have acquired the quietness of mind to receive it. For now we must conclude our little journey so that you may go on with your own and create for us a story from which we can all progress.

I don't understand.

We have answered a lot of your questions, and we hope our response has provided you with the stimulus to understand the nature of your creation and why you are here, but perhaps now it is time you answered a few questions of our own.

But you know everything that I know?

Yes but do you? The fact remains you have hidden more than you have allowed yourself to see.   Even we find it difficult to unravel the complexities you have put in place to shield you from your own reality, of who you really are and where it is you are going. However let us not delay any longer what it is you really wish to know and we shall endeavour to enlighten you with some facts. Perhaps then you will understand more clearly who we are and the real purpose for this communication.

The Chronicles of Kismah

In light of everything we have discussed I accept the fact that I create my own reality but like almost everyone else I'm not very good at it. Why is it so difficult to create the world we dream about?

Because you are still living the one you dreamed of at an earlier point.

So therefore I am obliged to follow a particular course and direction until I have finished what I started?

It is from a life you once dreamed that you are here now.

It's just a pity I cannot remember having the dream.

That is because you have not yet made good the opportunities available to you, but it is by no means the end of your journey. There will be other opportunities to create another life at another point in time, or if you prefer you could simply change the one you have now. The fact is you are still living the dream but your dilemma is you have not yet realised it. It may surprise you when I say I would like to have your dilemma. What I would not give to see the view of the hills that shadow you now as you write, or to desire what it is you think will bring you something you do not have.

But you can.

It may appear that way but it is only through you do I see what you can see.

But you look through my eyes?

Yes but I do not have the choice to look up and see the view outside your window.

Do you experience my joy?

I experience every moment of it, including all the joys you are unaware of, and I live every emotion as if it were my own.

And why am I not aware of these joys?

Because you are still imbued with the fear of survival and what might happen if you cannot maintain it, whereas I have no such concern. The fact is I feel everything you feel and desire the same things you desire because I know why it is you yearn for the things you think will make a difference. However we must accept our limitations for what they are and rejoice in the potentials of what they will become. I cannot affect how you think or the directions you will take to fulfil your potential but what I can do is help you make sense of what it is doing to you and when it is time to look elsewhere.

I suppose that is your cue for bringing about a conclusion to our communication by telling me it is now time to look elsewhere.

Our time is indeed coming to a close but it would disappoint me to finish what we have begun without addressing the issues that precipitated our communication in the first place.

I don't understand?

There is still something that troubles you?

Perhaps that is because I suspect this is the end of our journey, at least as far as this communication is concerned and I still feel something is missing.

It is only the end as you perceive it, and even though our communication will not have alleviated all your concerns, it has gone some way to answering many of the questions you sought?

Yes it has, and probably a lot more than I bargained for, but it has surprised me, and what will I do with it?

You needn't do anything if you prefer, yet you have an imaginative mind and so we suspect you will think of something. The most important thing is now you no longer have an excuse for wondering what it is you must do to finish what you have begun.

The difficulty with anything you attempt to finish in life is there is always a distraction or a temptation to go off in a completely different direction.

That is simply the nature of the system and one of the many challenges you have yourself chosen, but let us not forget why it is you chose them, or the many joys you will take from the experience when it is finished. It is only while you are lost in the pattern that it is not always so obvious, but we are hopeful, for you at least, it is the beginning of the end.

Then why do I not feel so optimistic?

Perhaps you are unaware of the probabilities you have created, but in time they will bring their own reward. Yet even though we are aware of the potentials sometimes it can be difficult for us also, particularly if the probability requires a specific input from us in order to bring it to fruition, but that is a challenge for us and one that will also bring its own reward.

What about when it is all finished?

For us it is already finished, but you have yet to catch up.

I don't understand.

There is an ending and in this our part is complete, but you have yet to translate it into a sequence of words that you understand.

And what will happen when I do catch up? Will it be different?

There is no moment that can repeat itself, so it will

always be different, but we suspect something else will have changed.

In what way will it have changed?

The same way that everything is changed by a certain action or response.

And from that action there is always a consequence?

Yes, however in this instance there is a difference. The fact is neither of us expected this communication, but it was our decision to act and respond to your dilemma, and therefore the consequences now lie with us.

Why is that?

We have responded in a way that has the potential to affect your area of the game, however it is how it might affect the area beyond yours that we are concerned. It is always our intention to assist you as best we can in order to help you maintain a particular course and direction, but it is not our intention to affect the course and direction of someone with whom we are not responsible.

Surely that must be a calculated risk you take with everything you do that is involved with this particular pattern of life.

Yes, but when that assistance is responsible for revealing certain elements of the pattern in which you are lost it has the potential to affect a great deal more than it was intended.

Isn't the course of human history littered with people and events that have affected more than they were ever meant to?

Yes, and it is also littered with an assortment of consequences in which many return again and again to try and make amends, or rectify the many courses and directions they have negatively altered.

Including all those we often hail as our saviours and demons?

Particularly those you regard as both your saviours and demons, but let us hope that in this transcript we have created neither, because there is only one course and direction we aspire to affect.

I still don't quite understand why this system of communication must come to an end?

Do you really not know the answer?

I have an inkling, or a suspicion about something but I suppose deep down I don't want to accept it.

That is because you do not wish to contemplate the element of finality, and yet the truth is you have been at this particular point for many years, but you have been reluctant to accept it for reasons you know only too well. As you are no doubt aware, it is as a result of this lasting dilemma that our communication has grown, and the reason it cannot continue is because in light of everything we have discussed regarding your course and direction it was never meant to begin. The fact is you have finished what you began many years ago, yet you have gone further than even we had expected. You see, unknown to your senses of perception and not yet appreciated you have achieved something very few have any real desire to repeat. You have actually seen a way out of the game, and that is even before you have given yourself a chance to play it. From this cycle you have completed everything you set out to achieve, yet the reason it does not require you to leave the arena is because you are still very much entwined in the course and direction of others with whom you are attached.

What did I set out to complete?

The answers to your own questions, from which you have developed a yearning to understand what it means to be human, but you have made such an intricate pattern from your desire for knowledge that now you do not know what to do without it.

Sometimes I am so inquisitive I feel like I could fill a dozen books.

And you would simply be repeating the questions you have already asked, and in our part we would be repeating the answers we have given. We could discuss the structure of atoms, or the sun and the moon, the pattern of space and the part you play in its illusion, but do you really want to know?

I feel like I want to know everything.

Then love what it is you are asking.

What do you mean?

Learn to love the sun and the moon, the pattern of space in which the structure of atoms are expressed, and above all learn to love the illusion. Without love there is no desire, and so how can you possibly know the answer to something you have no intention of understanding. Ask what it is you love and the answer will never be denied. You see it is not that we have responded to anything you have asked, we have simply made available an element of understanding upon which your focus is emotionally attached.

So what you are saying is that a major element to understanding is love?

It is the only element! Without love you would not be here, and despite the ease in which you lose yourself to the dream again and again, without love it is highly unlikely you will ever be able to leave.

In other words we must leave the same way we came in?

The only way you will leave is by relinquishing the attachments that hold you to believe that this is where you belong, because the only place where those attachments exist is the place in which they were acquired. Dream if you will of the sky and the mountains, of bodies and forms, and make from them everything you desire and aspire to be, but you will not see beyond them unless you accept there is something more. It is simply a matter of asking what would you have instead. Ask with love and it will be received but always know deep down what it is that you are asking. And from the difficulty you see in the paths of others and the worlds they create, their battles, their wars their love and hate, it is when they look up and see a world beyond their own will they begin to take sight of the reality they have always known.

We speak of love in many forms, of levels and intensity, of patterns and emotion, but the love we are referring to is that with which you can see who you are as opposed to who you think you have become. Think not of what you have become in shape or form, of compatibility and survival, or why it is that you compete and compare, then what is the world you see? Now ask yourself the one question that has the potential to see beyond the system that holds you so purposefully in its light, "Who would I not forgive?" and when there is nothing to be seen then it is certain you will see a glimpse of the reality you have replaced.

If it was God that you were seeking then let it be known he has been found, but know in your finding that he was never lost to begin with, nor could he ever be, because the reality is you could not dream without him, nor could we communicate with you now in a way that lets you know you are dreaming.

Sometimes you wish for what we are, what we see and what we can be, and we freely admit that we are not bound by the restrictions of this system that you have accepted, and yet the irony is that we wish for what you are. Through us you understand but in you we are more, and one day the dilemma that is ours will be yours to ponder, but hear us clearly when we say do not wish for this moment before it is time.

We aspire to grow as does everything in creation and that is what gives reasoning to our joy and intention, and with this you cannot fail to bring us what we desire, but as is the nature of expansion there is always a price for our need, because in every course and direction it is never quite as easy as it was before.

And so it is time to leave you with our final story but one that you will have to finish alone. You are sad and it is understandable, but it may surprise you to know that so are we, and you are also wondering why it is we leave no space for you to question. The fact is there is nothing more for you to ask, at least about anything you have any real desire to know the answer to.

Kismah the sleeping God has finally woken to chronicle his journey into the unknown void of his own desire, but now it is time he returned to his rest, until such moments arise that he should be recalled.

Now we leave you with some questions of our own, but once again we leave no space for you to answer, at least not today in this time and in this place. For this purpose there is a specific point we shall wait, and you will join us when you are ready, only not for a while at least, but we look forward with anticipation to the intricacies of your response. Yet do not think that in this completion we have abandoned you for there is in fact one of us who wishes to continue, but not for scrutiny or for any other eyes but your own.

So what are these questions we are to ask that may occupy your thoughts until it is time to join us and continue what we had originally set out before we were temporarily distracted by this pattern in which you are now lost? They are of course the questions that precipitated this journey together and which you have asked of everyone else but yourself. Who are you when you sleep, where do you go when you are awake, and above all others where are you from when you are neither asleep nor awake?

When you have your answers then you can be sure you

will know where to find us, and until that moment arrives it is indeed time to say goodbye.

We appreciate your acknowledgement of what we have given you, but our input is not really as great you imagine. We have played our part we admit, but let us not forget that these are the chronicles of Kismah the sleeping God, and despite the energy of his waking, or the validity of his words you can be sure that now we are finished he sleeps once more.

The End

Appendix

The People who Couldn't Die

Their planet was alive with a natural assortment of wildlife and fauna that reflected almost every shade and colour imaginable, with vast purple and green oceans interspersed with mountains and a diverse collection of forestation. Yet with the exception of a few elaborate cities that towered over the landscapes in which they were constructed, the surface of the planet was mostly untouched by physical intervention. Instead it formed the camouflage of a greater world hidden below in the form of deep canyons and landscapes that had been carved out over millions of years. Yet unlike the dark lifeless caverns on earth they were illuminated by the energy of natural glowing crystallised rocks that were an integral part of the environment.

There were many similarities in terms of your own appearance and likeness, except they were much taller with fine delicate features, however the major difference that accelerated their evolution over other species such as your own is they did not die or age in appearance beyond a certain point. The experience of death that is a natural occurrence of the human process, for them was something they did not comprehend.   Therefore all emotion associated with its outcome such as fear, loss and bereavement was almost absent from all forms of their existence.

Needless to say they were far in advance of your own society in terms of technology and discovery, and there was very little of their own environment they had not endeavoured to explore and understand.

They were wonderful creators full of invention and discovery, and not only were they fully conversed with the structure of atoms and particles, but they clearly understood the union between them, including the intricate forms they had bonded to create.

They had learnt to perceive and manipulate the invisible matter between everything that existed, including its relationship with the physical universe, and they could travel vast distances with very little hindrance or the difficulty with which you are aware.

They were extremely adept in the manipulation and alteration of energy, and often used it to experiment with the development and transformation of dead planets in order to diversify the evolution of various life forms.

They were imbued with an immense curiosity and desire to understand everything they could perceive, travelling huge distances in search of new forms and patterns of intelligence. Yet, despite their interest in the diversity of creation, communication with other worlds was rare. Not through any lack of intention or desire, but because the sheer depth of their technology only ever proved to affect the natural process of another's evolution.

In many instances of discovery, they were so far in advance of other worlds that often communication served only to invoke either worship or fear, and so therefore interest was rarely extended beyond the point of observation.

There were other highly developed and complex worlds of which they were aware, and in a few cases even more advanced than their own, however, the various ways in which each had evolved provided insurmountable differences to involve any form of interaction or communication.

They were imbued with an incredible curiosity for the structure of reality and experimented relentlessly with various forms of consciousness. They could observe certain points in their history and would explore alternative futures using an intricate network of probabilities and variation.

They had also evolved an acute sense of perception where sound and colour were interrelated, and so everything encountered in one corresponded with the other. They could often hear something before they could see it, which added a rich sense of experience and installed in them a deep appreciation of their surroundings.

Whether it was the flicker of a leaf or the rotation of a planet, everything emitted a sound and a vibration, an intricate song and dance that expressed either a purpose or a history, and all of it they could perceive and interact in a way you cannot understand.

Similarly in the way all forms are limited in the ranges of frequency with which they can hear it is also the same in which they perceived the world around them. However not only were they fully conversant with this knowledge, but they could alter their own frequency in such a way as not to be seen by certain life forms in order to observe and experience various patterns of their existence.

Although a highly developed verbal language formed part of their existence, their main source of communication was through a type of thought induced visual imagery, with colour, tone and even the depth of a line having relevance.

They were artists before they could read and created intricate and emphatic pictures with the same sense of importance and achievement as you write your books. Often, their most accomplished artists were their greatest teachers, for they clearly understood and recognised that a single image possessed the potential to convey a thousand symbols.

Compared to your own language, interaction and communication between them was a colourful and fulfilling experience. They could intricately explore in detail another's feelings or share a certain event that only one of them had actually encountered. Needless to say, the company of those who had returned from a long exploration of an unknown system were highly valued, as were the perceptions of the innocent because it enabled them to view a situation with an unbiased perspective. However, there was no specialness or ability they valued above another, except for a deep appreciation of the diversity and difference in all aspects of life and being.

The education of their young played a pivotal part in their existence, however, because of the extreme differences in the various levels of knowledge between their ages it took a great deal of time and patience.

The choice of teacher was a delicate process and depended greatly on the personality of the student, yet once chosen they would often stay with them throughout their development that would last the equivalent of many lifetimes.

Even the decision to teach was a major undertaking. In most instances it was a direction often chosen by the eldest members, and borne from the desire to enhance and explore new avenues of fulfilment.

Therefore, the teachers were often highly advanced in all aspects of their existence as well as having acquired a specialist understanding in certain areas of creation and exploration. In all cases, their varied interests were always matched with that of the student.

Methods of education did not follow any particular pattern but were specifically designed around each personality, their ability and preference, however, simulation in which actions and reactions were monitored formed a major part of learning.

The entire process was highly organised and encompassed a large assortment of subjects and knowledge. Some would spend what we consider to be entire lifetimes in the pursuit and accomplishment of a specific field, while others preferred to explore a broader spectrum until a certain level of understanding resonated. However, advancement and growth was always the aim.

The scope for individuality was broad, and great care was exercised in nurturing its potential, however, such was the diversity of endeavour this created within their civilisation, the bonding between personalities was exceptionally intricate and complex.

It would take the equivalent of several lifetimes to generate the feelings you associate as love, and even this was no guarantee of continuity. Yet once activated, the intensity of emotion and bond of union between them was without comparison and would last indefinitely.

The only exception to forming such a bond was through a shared experience of an extreme nature, however it always involved the threat of life, and in a society that did not understand the meaning of death, this was not a common occurrence. Therefore the whole aspect of love and union that you take for granted as being an integral part of your existence, for them it was a highly valued but extremely rare experience.

Similarly of value but also rare was the experience of laughter. The intensity of creation upon which most of their energy was expelled was so much a part of their existence; it was an emotion they rarely experienced. However, through great periods of their evolution they slowly grew to appreciate its importance as a tonic to relieve the concentrations of creation upon which their existence was based, but like the bonding of personalities, for them it was an extremely rare and difficult emotion to generate.

Through time and the narrowing of their technological advances, the importance of these two emotions would slowly grow and become the prime motivations for their existence, exploration and observation of other worlds.

Despite their understanding of time and space there existed a few patterns of activity beyond explanation, yet one in particular had become such a great source of interest, it impacted immensely on how they viewed themselves and the universe.

It took the form of a large pulsating star at the core of their known system. However, unlike a star, it emitted a constant wave of vibration that not only appeared to affect everything within a large radius, but also produced a frequency they recognised from the earliest beginnings of their creation.

All attempts to explore or penetrate the environment around the sphere were thwarted and repulsed by an energy field they were unable to comprehend. Space, matter and even time were affected and in ways which defied all their known laws and understanding.

They had discovered one of the frequencies it emitted was evident in all forms of existence regardless of shape, size or composition, however, the more complex the creation, the greater the attraction between the opposing forces, which in turn enhanced its ability to penetrate the field of energy. Even though the frequency was constant, the colours it induced upon their senses of perception was not.

As the desire for exploration and technology advanced, their interest and attraction towards the anomaly increased, particularly among the elders of their species. It appeared that the greater experience of the individual the greater the attraction between them and the anomaly which enabled them to penetrate further into the epicentre.

It was one of only a few constants they could not unlock, and its presence not only ignited their curiosity, but also had introduced them to a whole new area of discovery, as it invited them to look again at what they could already perceive.   Had they missed something?   Was there something about the universe and their existence they had failed to understand?

Despite their advances in exploration, their strength lay not in technology, but in their curiosity and constant desire to grow, expand and understand everything they could perceive. However, as an ancient species from the earliest beginnings of creation the potential to grow and explore new patterns of existence was becoming more difficult and challenging.

Slowly they became restless, and little by little the older generation of their species began to leave for other systems. Where they went exactly no one ever knew, except to say that they never came back.

The sense of loss towards these eminent fathers who had contributed so much towards the growth of their civilisation was immense; yet there was little they could do to stem their departure, except to hope that one day they might return.

Through time and this perception of stagnation they began to experiment with other forms of consciousness, until one day, by accident, they had managed to eradicate a portion of another's conscious memory. Although the effect was only temporary, when the subject regained full awareness it created in them an unusually rare form of elation and heightened excitement. They also observed that the personality of the individual had somehow been changed, not in a negative context, but in a form of renewed appreciation of their surroundings.

Through further experimentation and to their amazement they realised that the rare emotional response of the waking subject that had originally captured their attention was a common element of the process, while in others it appeared to have a significant affect on their perception. Although the experience did not alter in any way their sense of identity on return, it left a lasting and positive impression.

With time and further exposure they began to divert their attention from the after effects of the experience towards the actions of the personality during the periods of memory loss. It made for a fascinating insight into the variations of their species, from the alternative manner in which they perceived their environment to the way they would attempt to communicate with one another during the process.

They viewed the experiment as a form of induced sleep, and began to vary the process to include longer periods and the creation of new elaborate environments with which to observe the action and reaction of the subjects involved. It was here they encountered a setback that would become an integral part of the process. The longer the individual remained in the dream state, the longer and more complicated it became to regain full conscious awareness after the experience. However, the variation and quality of heightened emotion on return, although more complex and diverse, was exponentially greater.

They turned their attention to a planet in the earlier stages of its development on the periphery of their known system and embarked on an intricate program of diversity and evolution. They created new species and fauna and introduced existing elements from other systems and altered their DNA in order to adapt, accelerate and regulate the infant planet. After many attempts and minute adjustments they eventually managed to create a delicate self-supporting environment in which to observe their experiment in altered states of consciousness.

The whole process, from the initial creation, participation and evolution was a resounding success and began to accelerate once more their growth and propel their species towards a whole new direction of fulfilment.

Various changes were made to the environment to alter and adapt the illusion of reality in which they participated, but one in particular had such an affect that the entire process began to evolve into an entirely new direction that took them completely by surprise.

They realised that the most valued emotions of the experiment were realised when it was ended at a certain point in the process, and diminished thereafter. They then decided to implement a process in which various actions and reactions would deliberately result in the termination of the dream. The effect was almost immediate.

This one simple alteration suddenly instigated a new process of survival, which in turn created a massive amplification of the emotions involved. The first thing they observed in the participants was conflict, and in ways they could not have imagined. Although this in itself did not create an emotion they valued, the participants began to change the pattern of their personalities in order to try and form a bond and union with similar entities. This not only enhanced their potential to survive but increased their rate of success when a conflict ensued.

They became so creative in their acts of survival, that not only did they successfully prevent their termination, they began to terminate the lives of other species and affect the entire balance of their environment.

Again a number of changes were implemented in which termination was not only dependent on their survival from other species but from the entire environment. So successful had they become in their ability to adapt, integrate and adjust to their surroundings, the implemented changes did not last any length of time to make a difference. Another solution was to be sought.

After various attempts to alter the experiment, a radical idea was implemented in which the species, regardless of their ingenuity and success in delaying their return to full consciousness, would self terminate at a given point in their existence. In other words they altered the design of the whole system with a process in which all forms would age and die at various stages of their involvement.

The decision was ingenious because it not only solved the solution of re-awakening from the illusion but it invoked in the participants an incredible sense of emotional union that was both profound and immense. This was the rarest form of raw emotion they had ever encountered and was so incredibly complex that it began to attract the attention of other life forms from far and wide.

The entire concept was a resounding success and created for their species a whole new direction of growth and fulfilment, and despite various alterations to the design, the young planet in which their energies were directed would remain at the heart of their evolution.

Although a large proportion did not actively participate in the illusion, they involved themselves with various aspects of the project, from the environment to the introduction and alteration to the incredible array of species.   It was a delicate and ongoing process that required a great deal of energy and skill in order to maintain a specific balance in which all the life forms could flourish.

New specialities began to emerge in which they could exert their technology and expertise, yet despite their efforts and enthusiasm for the whole project, there was reluctance among the population to actually participate. The primary reason for this is that despite the temporary aspect of the dream, the whole process that enabled them to explore another facet of their being was extremely addictive.   Therefore the largest proportion of participation was with the young who did not yet have the experience to see this as a reason to abstain.

Their enthusiasm and the acknowledged benefits of participation sometimes was such that they would live longer in the dream than in full conscious awareness, but always in the knowledge that one-day they would awaken to the reality where they belonged.   Like everything else, in time it would cease to capture their awareness, but for the moment it provided so much opportunity to fulfil their potential there was little reason not to participate.

The challenge in which they developed the conscious awareness of their young was soon eradicated and the planet became the preferred choice of education. From its initial concept to the complexities of graduation it eventually became known as a compressed school of intense learning.

The formula allowed for great imagination and was taken to various other parts of their known system and copied. Each design made for interesting variations in patterns of growth and fulfilment but it was always to the mother planet, its creators and participants that they looked to for their inspiration.

Those who had completed the cycle emanated such incredible radiance they were revered by whoever they came into contact with. It inspired in them many things, but more than any other was the desire to be just like them.

For a long period it appeared they had finally solved the stagnation of their species, and although they had not entirely ended the migration of their oldest members to other systems, the new direction in which they could continue to grow had been significantly reduced.

However, as with all avenues of life, the lights of new exploration are only so bright until the sparkle of learning it provides begins to subside. In delaying their exodus they had succeeded in ways their original creators could never have imagined, yet in their constant desire to grow they had only held back what was for them an inevitable consequence of their expansion. As a species, which had been developed from the earliest moments of creation, in time their greatest act of design and ingenuity would finally prove to be their last.

The complexities involved with the young planet meant that graduation was a long process that involved numerous cycles and repetition before it ceased to provide any further potential. However the result was so diverse that when completed it changed altogether the participant's view of what was important. As they had long ago discovered, no matter how intense the drive for understanding and perfection, on completion it will always die. For them it seemed that the perfect world that you yourself aspire, a world without learning or emotion, is simply a world without meaning.

Soon the compressed school of learning that had so successfully held back their departure to other systems began to accelerate their evolution to such a degree that their depth of purpose and complexity became almost unrecognisable to those who had not experienced and graduated from the illusion.

They began to encourage the participation of other energy forms and strands of consciousness. They taught them various aspects of the pattern and for a while the energy required in helping them to adapt and integrate with the design created in them another direction of fulfilment. It interested them to observe and see it evolve differently, and that despite the integration of various different energy fields the result of graduation remained intact.

Content that the design upon which they had invested so much energy would continue without them they started to leave. The exodus was slow to begin with as many stayed to observe and see how their beloved designs would evolve with the participation of other energy forms, but quickly their attention subsided until one day it was noticed they had finally left.

Like the original exodus of their elders that had precipitated the creation of the planet, no one quite knew where they had gone. They had grown so much as a species and contributed so much to the planetary system in which other forms from far and wide participated that it was assumed they had finally passed through the anomaly. The truth is no one ever knew for sure except to say that they never came back, leaving only the intricate patterns that were to be shared and extended throughout the system as testimony to their existence.

The young planet continued to flourish, and despite the various minor changes and alterations required to maintain a balance between the species, the wonderfully intricate designs of energy and life that formed the environment remained very much the design of the original creators.

For those who would participate the dream would always end, and the illusion in which they explored the various emotional elements of love and laughter would cease to capture their imagination.

Like your own creators and those that created them, a time will come when the world no longer provides you with the opportunity to grow, and like your creators you too will follow them. Where exactly you cannot know, until that is the moment arrives.

Enjoy what you have, and indulge in the experience as you prefer, but always know that for the reasons it was designed you live in a dream and one day the dream will end. When that ending will arrive no one knows, except to say it is not something you should fear, so rejoice in what it is and what it will be, but do not wish for it before it is complete.

This is the pattern of evolution in which you are all a part

"A rising tide makes
many pearls."

Kismah

6128205R00125

Printed in Great Britain
by Amazon.co.uk, Ltd.,
Marston Gate.